MW00914468

The "I LOVE MY INSTANT POT®"

Affordable Meals

Recipe Book

From *Cold Start Yogurt* to *Honey Garlic Salmon*,
175 Easy, Family-Favorite Meals You Can Make for under $12

Aileen Clark of AileenCooks.com

Adams Media
New York   London   Toronto   Sydney   New Delhi

Adams Media
An Imprint of Simon & Schuster, Inc.
57 Littlefield Street
Avon, Massachusetts 02322

First Adams Media trade paperback edition October 2019

ADAMS MEDIA and colophon are trademarks of Simon & Schuster.

For information about special discounts for bulk purchases, please contact Simon & Schuster Special Sales at 1-866-506-1949 or business@simonandschuster.com.

The Simon & Schuster Speakers Bureau can bring authors to your live event. For more information or to book an event contact the Simon & Schuster Speakers Bureau at 1-866-248-3049 or visit our website at www.simonspeakers.com.

Interior design by Colleen Cunningham
Interior layout by Julia Jacintho
Photographs by James Stefiuk

Manufactured in the United States of America

10 9 8 7 6 5 4 3 2 1

Library of Congress Cataloging-in-Publication Data
Names: Clark, Aileen, author.
Title: The "I love my instant pot®" affordable meals recipe book / Aileen Clark of AileenCooks.com.
Description: Avon, Massachusetts: Adams Media, 2019.
Series: "I love my" series.
Includes index.
Identifiers: LCCN 2019023034 (print) | LCCN 2019023035 (ebook) | ISBN 9781507211137 (pb) | ISBN 9781507211144 (ebook)
Subjects: LCSH: Pressure cooking. | Smart cookers. | LCGFT: Cookbooks.
Classification: LCC TX840.P7 C49 2019 (print) | LCC TX840.P7 (ebook) | DDC 641.5/87--dc23
LC record available at https://lccn.loc.gov/2019023034
LC ebook record available at https://lccn.loc.gov/2019023035

ISBN 978-1-5072-1113-7
ISBN 978-1-5072-1114-4 (ebook)

Contents

Introduction

You may hear the word *affordable* and think of eating the same boring thing, day after day, of surviving on nothing but peanut butter and jelly and ramen. The truth is, making affordable meals does not have to be boring or repetitive. There are many ways you can save money while cooking flavorful dishes.

That is where the Instant Pot® comes in! This multifunctional kitchen powerhouse allows you to make delicious meals with little hands-on time and even allows for making both a side dish and main dish in the same pot! It's a pressure cooker, rice cooker, and slow cooker—all in one. We will show you how to make affordable and tasty meals that cost $12 or less to make.

You will love cooking with the Instant Pot® because you can start the recipe when you get home and then walk away to focus on other important things in your life. You will come back to a delicious meal ready for you that did not cost much to make.

This cookbook will offer many ways to create yummy recipes with less-expensive ingredients. It will also offer ways to make a few of your own kitchen staples at home to save

additional money. Think homemade Chicken Broth (see recipe in Chapter 3) and Refried Beans (see recipe in Chapter 4).

This Instant Pot® cookbook is made for both the experienced Instant Pot® user and the brand-new user. We teach you how to do everything—including what all of those function buttons mean and how to properly clean your Instant Pot®. And then we dig in to amazing recipes like Chicken Pot Pie Soup (see recipe in Chapter 3) and Mushroom Risotto (see recipe in Chapter 10).

You will learn new ways to use your Instant Pot® to its full potential while saving money. Inside, you will find 175 affordable recipes that cost $12 or less to make. The recipes range from Homemade Granola to Ham and Egg Breakfast Burritos (see recipes in Chapter 2) and Salsa Chicken Tacos (see recipe in Chapter 7) to Sweet and Spicy Meatloaf (see recipe in Chapter 8). There is also an entire dessert chapter that includes yummy recipes like Cherry Cobbler and Chocolate-Dipped Strawberries (see recipes in Chapter 11). So, bring this cookbook into your kitchen and get cooking with the Instant Pot®.

1

Cooking with an Instant Pot®

So, you've got a brand-new Instant Pot®. Now what? It can seem intimidating to use a new kitchen tool, but it will be totally worth it! This chapter will teach you how to test out your Instant Pot® with the water test, what all of the Instant Pot®–specific terminology means, and which important accessories to have on-hand. You'll also learn some practical tips on saving money on groceries and how the cost of each recipe has been calculated.

In addition to reading this chapter, it is also recommended to read the user's manual that comes with your Instant Pot®. Different models of the Instant Pot® work slightly different, so it is important to have as much knowledge as possible. This will ensure you make some delicious and affordable meals!

Parts of Your Instant Pot®

Let's start with discussing the different parts of the Instant Pot® and how they work. This will help you feel more confident in cooking with the Instant Pot®.

The Sealing Ring

The sealing ring fits snugly inside the lid. It should be removed after every use and washed with soap and water or in the top rack of the dishwasher. Sealing rings do need to be replaced from time to time. If the silicone begins to crack, it will need to be replaced as it is vital for pressure cooking with the Instant Pot®.

The Inner Pot

The inner cooking pot must always be used when using the Instant Pot®. It is dishwasher safe and should be cleaned after each use.

Pressure Release Valve

The pressure release valve is on top of the lid. It has two settings "Sealing" and "Venting." "Sealing" is used when cooking under pressure. "Venting" is used when slow cooking and when releasing pressure.

Antiblock Shield

The antiblock shield is a small round shield found on the inside of the lid. It prevents starchy foods like pasta from clogging the pressure release valve. It should be removed and washed often. To remove, hold onto the edge of the lid with both hands and push the side of the antiblock shield toward the edge of the lid with both thumbs.

Float Valve

The float valve is found next to the pressure release valve. It indicates whether the Instant Pot® is currently under pressure. When it is lifted up and slightly above the lid, the Instant Pot® is pressurized. When the float valve drops down, the Instant Pot® has depressurized.

Function Buttons

There are many function buttons on your Instant Pot®. They are preprogrammed buttons that cook your food for a set time. Press the button multiple times for different cook time options or use the +/- button to adjust the cook time to your liking. Following is a review of some of the most common buttons.

Manual/Pressure Cook Buttons

Many recipes require you to push the Manual or Pressure Cook button and adjust the cook time for the selected recipe. Different models of Instant Pot® have the button named differently. So, as long as you have either the Manual or Pressure Cook button, you are good to go. This button simply allows you to cook foods at high pressure and program a time using the +/- buttons.

Rice Button

The Rice button is a preprogrammed button with three settings: 12 minutes, 15 minutes, and 8 minutes. It exists for cooking white rice on low pressure.

Multigrain Button

The Multigrain button is made for brown and white rice. It cooks rice at high pressure for either 20 minutes, 40 minutes, or 60 minutes.

Sauté Button

The Sauté button is one of the greatest things about the Instant Pot®. It allows you to brown meats in your Instant Pot® before cooking them under pressure. This saves you on cleanup and allows you to cook without the need for a stove.

Keep in mind that after using the Sauté function, you will need to deglaze the bottom of your pot by pouring in water or broth and scraping off any food that is stuck to the bottom of the cooking pot. This allows the Instant Pot® to pressurize.

Slow Cook Button

You no longer need a separate slow cooker. The Instant Pot® functions as a slow cooker with this button. This button has 2½ hour and 4 hour preprogrammed times and allows the time to be adjusted with the +/- buttons. The Instant Pot® lid can be used or a regular glass lid may be used. The lid does not need to be locked in place as the pot will not be pressurizing and instead will be slow cooking.

BURN Notice

From time to time, you may end up with a BURN notice on the screen of your Instant Pot®. This indicates that there is either not enough liquid in the Instant Pot® for it to pressurize or there is food stuck to the bottom of the inner pot that is preventing the Instant Pot® from pressurizing. If this happens, release the pressure and open the lid. Use a spatula to remove any food stuck to the bottom of the pot and add ½ cup more liquid. Then just close the lid and restart the cooking process as described in the recipe.

To prevent the BURN notice from happening, make sure to deglaze your inner cooking pot with liquid after using the Sauté function. You should also make sure you are using at least 1 cup liquid for the mini and 6-quart models and 1½ cups of liquid for the 8-quart model. The liquid does not have to be water; any thin liquid will work.

Using the Lid and Releasing Pressure

When using the Instant Pot® to cook under pressure, the lid must be attached and locked in place in order for the Instant Pot® to work. You will know the lid is on because the Instant Pot® will chime at you—letting you know it has been successfully attached. The lid will then stay locked until the Instant Pot® has completed cooking and safely released the pressure from the machine.

Opening and Closing the Lid

To close the lid, align the triangle on the lid with the triangle on the Instant Pot® next to the unlocked lock, then turn the lid clockwise until secure. To open the lid, the Instant Pot® must have completely depressurized and the sealing valve must be turned to Venting. Turn the lid counterclockwise to open.

Natural Release (NR)

Natural Release refers to letting your Instant Pot® depressurize on its own. When your food finishes cooking, there is nothing you need to do. It will slowly release the pressure and the float valve will drop down when it's done. This takes anywhere from 5 to 40 minutes. Some recipes require a set time for Natural Release and then require a Quick Release. This method is recommended when cooking rice, beans, and meat.

Quick Release (QR)

Quick release is used to manually depressurize the Instant Pot®. It can be done by turning the pressure release valve to Venting. This will release hot steam from the top of the valve. Make sure your hand is not over the valve when turning it to Venting. Instead, turn it from the side of the valve. This method is recommended for recipes that include pasta, which can easily overcook.

The Water Test

The first thing you need to do with your new Instant Pot® is a water test. This ensures your Instant Pot® is working properly and gets you oriented with the machine. Here is what to do:

1 Plug in your Instant Pot®. Make sure the cord on the pot side is fully connected.

2 Place the inner pot inside the Instant Pot® and add 3 cups of water. Make sure the silicone ring is securely in place under the lip of the Instant Pot® lid. Close the lid on your Instant Pot®.

3 Push the pressure release valve to Sealing. This happens automatically if using the Ultra model.

4 Press the Steam button and use the +/- buttons until you get to 2. For the Ultra model, use the dial to turn to steam and set to 2 minutes. Press Start.

5 After 10 seconds, your Instant Pot® will beep and the time will go away. It will take several minutes for the Instant Pot®

to pressurize. Once the Instant Pot® has pressurized, the float valve will pop up and the Instant Pot® will begin to count down from 2.

6   Once it's done counting down, it will switch to Keep Warm mode and being counting up from when the Instant Pot® finished cooking. It will also begin to depressurize.

7   Release the pressure with a quick release by turning the pressure release valve from Sealing to Venting. (For the Ultra model: Press the Quick Pressure Release button.) It will take a few minutes for all of the steam and pressure to release. Once it's done, you will hear the float valve drop.

8   Open your pot—you have officially completed your water test and you are ready to get cooking!

Cleaning the Instant Pot®

It is important to keep your Instant Pot® clean and store it with the inner pot inside of the Instant Pot® when not in use. This prevents the accidental cooking without the inner pot—which will ruin your machine.

To clean your Instant Pot®, wipe down the outside of the Instant Pot® with a damp towel. The lid, inner cooking pot, and sealing ring are all dishwasher safe. The lid and sealing ring are top rack only.

In addition to cleaning the lid and inner pot, the antiblock shield and pressure release valve should be cleaned from time to time either by hand or in a dishwasher-safe container that prevents them from falling down into the heating element of the dishwasher.

Pot-in-Pot Cooking

Some recipes call for pot-in-pot cooking. This refers to cooking two different items in the Instant Pot® at the same time. You don't have to have a recipe state this to try this method. Just find two recipes with the same cook time and place one above the other on a trivet.

Foil Sling

A foil sling is used for many pot-in-pot recipes. Make a foil sling with a (2') piece of foil folded lengthwise into thirds. Place it underneath a cake pan or other pot-in-pot pan and use it to carefully lower the pan into the Instant Pot®. Fold the ends of the foil sling over the top of the pot and use those pieces of foil to remove the pan when cooking is finished.

Accessories for the Instant Pot®

There are several accessories for the Instant Pot® that are used in this cookbook. Not all recipes require an accessory but these are our favorite go-to accessories for the recipes that do need them.

Silicone Muffin Cups

Silicone muffin cups work wonderfully when making egg muffins in the Instant Pot® or handheld foods like Mini Meatloaves (see recipe in Chapter 8) and Mini Pumpkin Cheesecakes (see recipe in Chapter 11).

7" Cake Pan

The 7" cake pan is used to make both casseroles and cakes that need to keep their shape but can't sit directly in the cooking liquid.

7" PushPan

The 7" PushPan is very important for making cheesecakes in the Instant Pot®. If you want to make these deliciously creamy desserts, then you will want to have a PushPan on hand.

6-Cup Metal Bowl

Like the cake pan, the metal bowl is used to hold foods that can't sit directly in the cooking liquid. It's wonderful for recipes that won't fit in the cake pan like Sweet Corn Tamalito (see recipe in Chapter 6).

6-Cup Bundt Pan

The Bundt pan is used to make dishes look prettier and more appetizing. You will find recipes in this book like Sour Cream Coffee Cake (see recipe in Chapter 2) and Corn Bread (see recipe in Chapter 6) that are cooked in a Bundt pan.

Ramekins

Like silicone muffin cups, ramekins are used to cook individual portions of recipes. They are slightly larger and can be wrapped in foil and cooked directly on the steam rack or in the bottom of the Instant Pot®.

Trivet

The trivet comes with your Instant Pot®. Make sure to keep it on hand because it is used for many recipes.

Steamer Basket

The steamer basket works well for steaming vegetables and for pot-in-pot cooking when cooking something in the bottom of the pot (like potatoes) and cooking something on top (like meatloaf).

How to Save Money on Groceries

You probably purchased this Instant Pot® cookbook because you want to save money on groceries while still making delicious food. Well, you are in the right place. This book has many recipes that use inexpensive ingredients to make delicious and filling meals. There are also two rules for saving money on groceries that you should focus on when using this cookbook: planning your meals and not wasting ingredients.

Plan Your Meals

The best way to plan your meals is to take an inventory of your pantry and plan your meals around the ingredients you already have on hand. Plan out what you will cook for each meal for the entire week—leaving a day here or there to eat up any leftovers you may have or for unexpected nights out. Be sure to write down your meal plan. If it is not in writing, you will likely forget or not stick with the plan.

Once you have an inventory of your current pantry and refrigerator items, make a grocery list of the additional items you need to make your meals. This will prevent you from having three half-used bags of rice and inspire you to use up the rest of the pasta you bought last month and forgot about. If you do find multiple packages of the same item, use the one that is set to expire first.

Another great way to save money while planning your meals is checking the weekly grocery flyers to see which items are on sale. You will get the most bang for your buck by planning around the meat and produce sales. Simply figure out which items are on sale and plan your dinners around those items and the items you already have on hand. This can save a lot of money if the time is made to plan for it.

If possible, try ordering your groceries online and picking them up at the store. Many retailers now offer this service and it can save a lot of money on impulse purchases. If you are not walking around the store than you are less likely to buy something extra on impulse.

Coupons

If you do end up shopping in-store, make sure you check a coupon app for the items on your list. There are many coupon apps out there that allow you to select rebates on popular coupon items and scan your receipt after purchase. Once you reach a certain threshold (anywhere from $5 to $20), the app will send you a check. Use that money toward future grocery purchases. Some great apps for cash back on groceries are: SavingStar, Ibotta, and Checkout 51.

If you want to use actual coupons in-store, try *Coupon Sherpa* or Coupons. com. Both of these websites show coupons available for in-store savings. *Coupon Sherpa* allows coupons to be scanned directly from your smartphone and Coupons.com lets you link the coupons to your store's loyalty card.

Buy in Bulk

Purchasing in bulk is another great way to save money, if done right. Start by making a list of the ingredients you use every single week and purchase regularly. For many, it's meat like ground beef. Next,

determine if you have extra room to store bulk items—pantry space for dry goods or freezer space for meat. Lastly, price check your local grocery store prices on the same item before buying in bulk (many grocery stores will show you prices online).

Not all bulk purchases are a better deal, so it's important this is done before heading to your local bulk store. If you can check off all three of these items, then set some money aside to buy in bulk. It will save you money in the long run.

Don't Waste Ingredients

Now comes the fun part, the cooking! Being a frugal cook takes some practice. The hardest part for many people is actually making what you planned and not wasting those ingredients. A great way to ensure this happens is by pulling out all of the nonperishable items you need for that day's recipe and leaving them on your counter in the morning (or even the night before). It's a great visual reminder to get cooking and not waste the food you purchased.

Another helpful tool is a magnetic dry-erase board with the week's meal plan hanging on your refrigerator. That way you will see it every time you open your refrigerator.

If at the end of the week you find yourself with leftover ingredients, get creative and use them up. Don't let them go to waste. You could repurpose them into a new meal or simply freeze them until you can use them. Most things can be frozen if packaged properly. Just make sure you create a label for them (wet erase markers are perfect for this) so you don't forget what it is you froze. Then add those ingredients to your inventory for the next week's meal plan.

How the Recipe Costs Are Calculated

You will see that every recipe in this cookbook has a cost included. The recipes are calculated by the portion of ingredients used (e.g., 1 teaspoon dried parsley), not the entire package. The recipe costs are based on a national food retailer's prices and are accurate at the time of publication.

2

Breakfast

Breakfast in the Instant Pot® is wonderful if you want to be better about eating breakfast but never seem to have a lot of time in the morning. Many of the recipes in this chapter can be used to make breakfasts ahead of time or can be set up to cook while you get ready for the day. There are sweet recipes like Monkey Bread and Overnight French Toast Casserole, along with heartier options like Denver Omelet Egg Muffins and Sausage and Egg Sandwiches.

Monkey Bread

Enjoy a special treat in under an hour with this recipe for monkey bread made in the Instant Pot®. Monkey Bread is a pull-apart–style bread coated in cinnamon sugar and drizzled with vanilla icing. It tastes like a cinnamon roll with less work and more fun!

- **Total Recipe Cost: $3.09**
- **Hands-On Time:** 15 minutes
- **Cook Time:** 23 minutes

Serves 4

2½ cups all-purpose flour
4 teaspoons baking powder
½ teaspoon salt
1 cup unsalted butter, chilled and divided
1 cup plus 2 teaspoons whole milk, divided
1 cup granulated sugar
3 tablespoons ground cinnamon
½ cup packed light brown sugar
1½ cups water
½ cup powdered sugar
½ teaspoon vanilla extract

MONKEY BREAD

Monkey Bread got its name because it is a finger food that one would pick apart like a monkey. This pastry is known by many other names, including: golden dumpling coffee cake, monkey puzzle bread, Hungarian coffee cake, and sticky bread.

1. Spray a 6-cup Bundt pan with cooking spray and set aside.

2. In a medium bowl, whisk together flour, baking powder, and salt.

3. Cut ½ cup butter into small cubes and place into dry ingredients. Use a fork to mix in the butter until dry ingredients are crumbly and about the size of peas.

4. Slowly pour in 1 cup milk, mixing until a dough forms. Use clean hands to knead the dough about 10 minutes until smooth.

5. Pour dough onto a lightly floured surface and pat into a 10" round.

6. Cut dough up into 1" pieces and set aside.

7. In a gallon-sized zip-top bag, combine granulated sugar and cinnamon. Close bag and shake to mix.

8. Place cut pieces of dough into bag of cinnamon sugar. Gently knead bag until each piece of dough is coated in cinnamon sugar. Remove dough pieces and arrange evenly in greased Bundt pan.

9. Set Instant Pot® to Sauté. Pour in brown sugar and remaining ½ cup butter. Whisk until butter is melted and brown sugar is dissolved, about 2 minutes.

10. Turn off Instant Pot®. Pour butter mixture over the top of Monkey Bread pieces in Bundt pan.

continued on next page

Monkey Bread (continued)

11 Clean inner pot and place back inside Instant Pot®.

12 Add 1½ cups water to Instant Pot® and place a trivet inside Instant Pot®.

13 Cover Bundt pan with a paper towel and foil. Crimp edges to discourage water from getting inside pan.

14 Create a foil sling and carefully lower Bundt pan into the Instant Pot®. Close lid and set pressure release to Sealing.

15 Press Manual or Pressure Cook button and adjust time to 21 minutes.

16 When the timer beeps, allow pressure to release naturally for 5 minutes and then quick release remaining pressure. Unlock lid and remove it.

17 Remove Bundt pan using foil sling. Remove foil and paper towel from the top of pan and let cool on a rack 5 minutes.

18 Make vanilla icing while Monkey Bread is cooling. In a small bowl, whisk together powdered sugar, remaining 2 teaspoons milk, and vanilla. Set aside.

19 Turn Bundt pan over onto a plate and wiggle pan to allow bread to release.

20 Drizzle Monkey Bread with vanilla icing while it is still warm. Enjoy immediately and store any unused portion in an air-tight container at room temperature up to three days.

PER SERVING

CALORIES: 1,107 | **FAT:** 49g | **PROTEIN:** 11g | **SODIUM:** 698mg
FIBER: 5g | **CARBOHYDRATES:** 161g | **SUGAR:** 95g

Sour Cream Coffee Cake

Coffee cake is such a delicious treat with a cup of tea or coffee. It can be made ahead of time and frozen. Simply let it cool and wrap it in two layers of foil. When you are ready to serve the coffee cake, remove it from the freezer, unwrap, and let it defrost at room temperature for about 2 hours. Slices may be reheated individually or eaten at room temperature.

- **Total Recipe Cost:** $3.08
- **Hands-On Time:** 15 minutes
- **Cook Time:** 25 minutes

Serves 6

1⅓ cups all-purpose flour, divided
1 cup granulated sugar
1 teaspoon salt, divided
½ teaspoon ground cinnamon
1 teaspoon baking powder
1 cup plus 1 tablespoon unsalted butter, divided
½ cup full-fat sour cream
1 large egg
½ teaspoon vanilla extract
½ cup packed light brown sugar
1½ cups water

1. Grease a 6-cup Bundt pan with cooking spray and set aside.

2. In a large bowl, whisk together 1 cup flour, granulated sugar, ½ teaspoon salt, cinnamon, and baking powder.

3. Soften ½ cup butter. Cut remaining butter into cubes and chill for later.

4. In a medium bowl, whisk ½ cup softened butter, sour cream, egg, and vanilla together until fluffy.

5. Fold wet ingredients into dry ingredients. This is your coffee cake batter.

6. In a separate medium bowl, combine remaining cubed butter, ⅓ cup flour, and brown sugar. Use a fork to mix it until it is crumbly and roughly the size of peas. This is your streusel.

7. Pour half of the streusel into Bundt pan. Pour half of the coffee cake batter on top of streusel in Bundt pan. Repeat with remaining streusel and coffee cake batter.

8. Top Bundt pan with a paper towel and a piece of foil, crimped around the edges of the pan.

9. Pour water into Instant Pot® and add trivet.

10. Create a foil sling and carefully lower the covered Bundt pan into the Instant Pot®. Close lid and set pressure release to Sealing.

continued on next page

Sour Cream Coffee Cake (continued)

11 Press Manual or Pressure Cook button and adjust time to 25 minutes.

12 When the timer beeps, allow pressure to release naturally and then unlock lid and remove it. Then carefully remove coffee cake using the foil sling. Remove paper towel and foil.

13 Let cool on a rack 10 minutes and then remove the coffee cake from the Bundt pan by turning it over onto a plate. Let cool fully.

14 Store in an air-tight container at room temperature up to three days.

PER SERVING

CALORIES: 482 | **FAT:** 20g | **PROTEIN:** 4g | **SODIUM:** 473mg
FIBER: 1g | **CARBOHYDRATES:** 74g | **SUGAR:** 52g

Chocolate Chip Banana Bread

Whip up a batch of this Chocolate Chip Banana Bread in your Instant Pot®. It comes out sweet, dense, and moist every time.

- **Total Recipe Cost: $2.82**
- **Hands-On Time: 15 minutes**
- **Cook Time: 65 minutes**

Serves 6

1¾ cups all-purpose flour
½ cup granulated sugar
½ cup packed light brown sugar
1 teaspoon baking soda
½ teaspoon salt
½ teaspoon ground cinnamon
2 large eggs, lightly beaten
½ cup melted unsalted butter, cooled slightly
½ cup buttermilk
1 teaspoon vanilla extract
1½ cups mashed banana (about 3 bananas)
1 cup mini semisweet chocolate chips
1 cup water

HOW TO QUICKLY RIPEN BANANAS

Use this simple trick to quickly ripen bananas in the oven. Preheat oven to 400°F. Place unripened bananas on a foil-lined baking pan. Heat bananas in oven 20 minutes, flipping once. Bananas will come out with black skins and soft, sweet fruit. Let cool before baking into bread.

1 In a large bowl, whisk together flour, granulated sugar, brown sugar, baking soda, salt, and cinnamon.

2 In a medium bowl, whisk together eggs, butter, buttermilk, and vanilla.

3 Make a well in the center of dry ingredients and mix in wet ingredients. The batter should still be lumpy with a few dry spots.

4 Fold in mashed banana and chocolate chips.

5 Grease a 7″ PushPan with oil and flour.

6 Pour banana bread batter into PushPan. Place a paper towel on top of pan and tightly cover with foil.

7 Pour water into Instant Pot® and add trivet. Gently lower the PushPan into Instant Pot® using the foil sling. Close lid and set pressure release to Sealing.

8 Press Manual or Pressure Cook button and adjust time to 65 minutes.

9 When the timer beeps, quick release pressure, unlock lid, and carefully remove bread using the foil sling. Remove foil and paper towel. Use a clean paper towel to gently blot up any additional moisture that may have accumulated on top of Chocolate Chip Banana Bread.

10 Let cool on a cooling rack 10 minutes. Carefully remove the Chocolate Chip Banana Bread using push feature in pan.

11 Store in an air-tight container up to three days.

PER SERVING

CALORIES: 627 | FAT: 27g | PROTEIN: 8g | SODIUM: 460mg
FIBER: 4g | CARBOHYDRATES: 95g | SUGAR: 58g

Overnight French Toast Casserole

All the magic happens with this French toast casserole overnight. The crusty French bread soaks in the egg mixture making a delightful custard that cooks up perfectly in the morning. The bread type is important for this recipe. A less crusty bread will fall apart and not have the chewy texture that makes Overnight French Toast Casserole so delicious.

- **Total Recipe Cost:** $4.90
- **Hands-On Time:** 10 minutes
- **Cook Time:** 30 minutes

Serves 5

½ loaf (day-old) French bread, cut into 1" chunks
8 large eggs
¾ cup whole milk
3 tablespoons granulated sugar
3 tablespoons packed light brown sugar
1 teaspoon vanilla extract
1 teaspoon ground cinnamon
½ teaspoon salt
2 tablespoons unsalted butter, cubed and chilled
1½ cups water
¼ cup maple syrup

1 Grease a 7" cake pan with cooking spray.

2 Arrange chunks of French bread in a single layer on bottom of pan.

3 In a medium bowl, whisk together eggs, milk, granulated sugar, brown sugar, vanilla, cinnamon, and salt until fully combined. Pour egg mixture over French bread.

4 Sprinkle cubed butter on top of French bread. Refrigerate, at least 2 hours, or overnight.

5 Pour water into Instant Pot®. Place a trivet inside.

6 Place a paper towel on top of cake pan and tightly cover with foil. Create a foil sling and use it to gently lower pan into Instant Pot®.

7 Close lid and set pressure release to Sealing.

8 Press Manual or Pressure Cook button and adjust time to 30 minutes.

9 When the timer beeps, allow pressure to release naturally for 10 minutes and then quick release remaining pressure. Unlock lid and remove it.

10 Carefully remove French toast casserole using foil sling. Remove foil and paper towel.

11 Serve topped with maple syrup.

PER SERVING

CALORIES: 411 | FAT: 15g | PROTEIN: 16g | SODIUM: 650mg
FIBER: 1g | CARBOHYDRATES: 54g | SUGAR: 30g

Apple Pie Oatmeal

Apple Pie Oatmeal made in the Instant Pot® is a delicious way to start the day. This recipe calls for Gala apples, but any variety of apple may be used. Keep in mind that the sweetness of the apples will affect the overall sweetness of the oatmeal.

- **Total Recipe Cost:** $4.28
- **Hands-On Time:** 3 minutes
- **Cook Time:** 5 minutes

Serves 4

3 cups water

1½ cups diced Gala apples, divided

1 cup steel cut oats

1 tablespoon packed light brown sugar

3 teaspoons apple pie spice, divided

⅛ teaspoon salt

1 Combine water, 1 cup apples, oats, brown sugar, 2 teaspoons apple pie spice, and salt in Instant Pot®. Close lid and set pressure release to Sealing.

2 Press Manual or Pressure Cook button and adjust time to 5 minutes.

3 When the timer beeps, allow pressure to release naturally for 10 minutes and then quick release remaining pressure. Unlock lid and remove it.

4 Top with remaining apples and apple pie spice, and serve.

PER SERVING

CALORIES: 212 | FAT: 3g | PROTEIN: 7g | SODIUM: 74mg
FIBER: 7g | CARBOHYDRATES: 40g | SUGAR: 8g

Blueberry Oatmeal

Cooking steel cut oats in the Instant Pot® takes a lot less time than it does on the stovetop. The Instant Pot® makes it easy to enjoy an oatmeal breakfast made with steel cut oats on a busy day.

- **Total Recipe Cost: $2.64**
- **Hands-On Time: 3 minutes**
- **Cook Time: 5 minutes**

Serves 4

3 cups water

1½ cups frozen blueberries, divided

1 cup steel cut oats

1 tablespoon light brown sugar

⅛ teaspoon salt

½ teaspoon ground cinnamon

1 Combine water, 1 cup blueberries, oats, brown sugar, and salt in Instant Pot®. Close lid and set pressure release to Sealing.

2 Press Manual or Pressure Cook button and adjust time to 5 minutes.

3 When the timer beeps, allow pressure to release naturally for 10 minutes and then quick release remaining pressure. Unlock lid and remove it.

4 Top with cinnamon and remaining ½ cup blueberries and serve.

PER SERVING

CALORIES: 214 | FAT: 3g | PROTEIN: 7g | SODIUM: 74mg
FIBER: 7g | CARBOHYDRATES: 40g | SUGAR: 8g

STEEL CUT OATS VERSUS ROLLED OATS

It is important to select steel cut oats when cooking in the Instant Pot®. Steel cut oats take a significantly longer time to cook than rolled oats or quick-cooking oats. Rolled oats would become mushy if cooked in the Instant Pot® but steel cut oats come out perfectly chewy and not mushy at all while still cooking faster when pressure cooked. This is why steel cut oats are perfect for the Instant Pot®. They cook quickly with very little hands-on time.

Easy-Peel Hard-Boiled Eggs

Hard-boiled eggs are one of the easiest and most affordable breakfast options available. They are simple to make in the Instant Pot® and the 5–5–5 method shared in this recipe makes the shells very easy to peel.

- **Total Recipe Cost:** $1.20
- **Hands-On Time:** 5 minutes
- **Cook Time:** 5 minutes

Serves 6

1½ cups water
6 large eggs

1 Pour water into Instant Pot®. Place a trivet inside Instant Pot® and arrange eggs on top of trivet. Close lid and set pressure release to Sealing.

2 Press Manual or Pressure Cook button and adjust time to 5 minutes.

3 When the timer beeps, allow pressure to release naturally for 5 minutes and then quick release remaining pressure. Unlock lid and remove it.

4 Carefully place eggs into a bowl of ice water. Leave in ice bath 5 minutes.

5 Remove eggs, peal, and enjoy. Refrigerate any unpeeled eggs up to five days.

PER SERVING

CALORIES: 71 | FAT: 5g | PROTEIN: 6g | SODIUM: 71mg
FIBER: 0g | CARBOHYDRATES: 0g | SUGAR: 0g

Sausage and Cheddar Egg Muffins

These tasty egg muffins are easy to make with a few simple ingredients. If you don't have links on hand then sausage patties may be used.

- **Total Recipe Cost: $2.36**
- **Hands-On Time: 10 minutes**
- **Cook Time: 5 minutes**

Serves 4

4 large eggs
2 tablespoons whole milk
¼ teaspoon salt
⅛ teaspoon black pepper
2 precooked breakfast
    sausage links, sliced
2 tablespoons sharp
    Cheddar cheese
1½ cups water

1 Spray four silicone muffin cups with cooking spray and set aside.

2 In a small bowl, whisk together eggs, milk, salt, and pepper. Evenly distribute egg mixture into four muffin cups.

3 Evenly divide sausages and drop into egg mixture. Top each with ½ tablespoon cheese.

4 Pour water into Instant Pot® and add trivet.

5 Place filled muffin cups inside of a 7" cake pan. Top pan with a paper towel and a piece of foil crimped around the edges.

6 Create a foil sling and gently lower pan into Instant Pot® so it sits on top of trivet. Fold foil sling over pan.

7 Close lid and set pressure release to Sealing.

8 Press Manual or Pressure Cook button and adjust time to 5 minutes.

9 When the timer beeps, let pressure release naturally for 2 minutes and then quick release remaining pressure. Unlock lid and remove it. Remove pan from Instant Pot® using foil sling.

10 Remove foil from the top of muffin cups and then carefully remove egg muffins. Enjoy immediately.

PER SERVING

CALORIES: 124 | FAT: 9g | PROTEIN: 10g | SODIUM: 333mg
FIBER: 0g | CARBOHYDRATES: 1g | SUGAR: 1g

Denver Omelet Egg Muffins

Like a Denver omelet in muffin form, these easy egg muffins are perfect for an on-the-go breakfast. They can be made ahead of time and reheated in the morning with just 30 seconds in the microwave.

- **Total Recipe Cost:** $5.73
- **Hands-On Time:** 10 minutes
- **Cook Time:** 5 minutes

Serves 4

4 large eggs
2 tablespoons whole milk
¼ teaspoon salt
⅛ teaspoon black pepper
4 tablespoons diced ham
2 tablespoons diced onion
2 tablespoons diced green
  bell pepper
2 tablespoons sharp
  Cheddar cheese
1½ cups water

1 Spray four silicone muffin cups with cooking spray and set aside.

2 In a small bowl, whisk together eggs, milk, salt, and pepper. Evenly distribute egg mixture into four muffin cups.

3 Evenly divide up ham, onion, and bell pepper and drop equal amounts into each filled muffin cup.

4 Top each with ½ tablespoon cheese.

5 Pour water into Instant Pot® and add trivet.

6 Place filled muffin cups inside of a 7″ cake pan. Top pan with a paper towel and a piece of foil crimped around the edges.

7 Create a foil sling and gently lower pan into Instant Pot® so it sits on top of trivet. Fold foil sling over pan. Close lid and set pressure release to Sealing.

8 Press Manual or Pressure Cook button and adjust time to 5 minutes.

9 When the timer beeps, let pressure release naturally for 2 minutes and then quick release remaining pressure. Unlock lid and remove it. Remove pan from Instant Pot® using foil sling.

10 Remove foil from the top of muffin cups and then carefully remove egg muffins. Enjoy immediately and refrigerate any leftovers.

PER SERVING

CALORIES: 117 | FAT: 8g | PROTEIN: 10g | SODIUM: 175mg
FIBER: 0g | CARBOHYDRATES: 2g | SUGAR: 1g

Bacon and Chive Egg Muffins

Take this classic breakfast combination and make it into an easy handheld breakfast. The egg mixture may be prepared the night before and refrigerated. Let it sit at room temperature for 10 minutes prior to cooking in the Instant Pot®.

- **Total Recipe Cost:** $2.93
- **Hands-On Time:** 10 minutes
- **Cook Time:** 5 minutes

Serves 4

4 large eggs
2 tablespoons whole milk
¼ teaspoon salt
⅛ teaspoon black pepper
2 slices cooked bacon, crumbled
2 tablespoons diced chives
2 tablespoons sharp Cheddar cheese
1½ cups water

1 Spray four silicone muffin cups with cooking spray and set aside.

2 In a small bowl, whisk together eggs, milk, salt, and pepper. Evenly distribute egg mixture into muffin cups.

3 Evenly divide up bacon and chives and drop equal amounts onto each egg muffin.

4 Top each with ½ tablespoon cheese.

5 Pour water into Instant Pot®. Place trivet inside.

6 Place filled muffin cups inside of a 7" cake pan. Top pan with a paper towel and a piece of foil crimped around the edges. Create a foil sling and gently lower pan into Instant Pot® so it sits on top of trivet. Fold foil sling over pan.

7 Close lid and set pressure release to Sealing.

8 Press Manual or Pressure Cook button and adjust time to 5 minutes.

9 When the timer beeps, let pressure release naturally for 2 minutes and then quick release remaining pressure. Unlock lid and remove it. Remove pan from Instant Pot® using foil sling.

10 Remove foil from the top of muffin cups and then carefully remove egg muffins. Enjoy immediately and refrigerate any leftovers.

PER SERVING

CALORIES: 113 | FAT: 8g | PROTEIN: 9g | SODIUM: 311mg
FIBER: 0g | CARBOHYDRATES: 1g | SUGAR: 1g

Ham and Egg Breakfast Burritos

An easy and tasty breakfast burrito recipe that can be easily customized with your choice of precooked breakfast meat.

- **Total Recipe Cost:** $2.82
- **Hands-On Time:** 5 minutes
- **Cook Time:** 4 minutes

Serves 4

4 large eggs
⅛ cup whole milk
¼ teaspoon salt
⅛ teaspoon black pepper
½ cup diced ham
1 tablespoon butter
4 (10") flour tortillas
4 tablespoons salsa
¼ cup grated Mexican-blend cheese

FREEZING BREAKFAST BURRITOS

Breakfast burritos can be made in bulk and frozen for a quick and tasty breakfast. Prepare breakfast burritos and let them cool to room temperature. Wrap each burrito in foil and place in a zip-top freezer-safe bag. When ready to eat, remove a single burrito from the freezer and unwrap foil. Cook in the microwave at 50 percent power for 2½ minutes until warm in the center.

1 In a small bowl, whisk together eggs, milk, salt, and pepper. Mix in ham.

2 Press Sauté button on Instant Pot®. Add in butter and let melt. Once butter is melted, pour in egg mixture and ham.

3 Cook and stir eggs 3 minutes until no longer runny.

4 Divide egg scramble evenly among four tortillas.

5 Spread salsa on eggs and top with cheese. Roll into burritos and enjoy immediately or freeze.

PER SERVING

CALORIES: 369 | FAT: 17g | PROTEIN: 16g | SODIUM: 960mg
FIBER: 3g | CARBOHYDRATES: 38g | SUGAR: 4g

Veggie Breakfast Burritos

A healthier take on the traditional breakfast burrito. Although these burritos are meatless, the mushrooms take on a meaty texture that fills you up.

- **Total Recipe Cost: $3.10**
- **Hands-On Time: 5 minutes**
- **Cook Time: 6 minutes**

Serves 4

4 large eggs
⅛ cup whole milk
¼ teaspoon salt
⅛ teaspoon black pepper
1 tablespoon butter
2 tablespoons diced onion
2 tablespoons diced red bell pepper
⅛ cup chopped mushrooms
4 (10") flour tortillas
4 tablespoons salsa
¼ cup grated Mexican-blend cheese

1 In a small bowl, whisk together eggs, milk, salt, and pepper.

2 Press Sauté button on Instant Pot®. Add in butter and let melt. Once butter is melted, pour in onion, bell pepper, and mushrooms. Cook 1 minute until onions are soft.

3 Pour in egg mixture and continue to cook 3 more minutes until eggs are no longer runny.

4 Divide egg scramble evenly among four tortillas.

5 Spread salsa on eggs and top with cheese. Roll into burritos and enjoy immediately or freeze.

PER SERVING

CALORIES: 361 | FAT: 16g | PROTEIN: 15g | SODIUM: 958mg
FIBER: 3g | CARBOHYDRATES: 39g | SUGAR: 5g

Cheesy Hash Brown Casserole

This casserole can be made ahead of time and refrigerated before cooking. When you are ready, take it out of the refrigerator and cook in the Instant Pot® as directed.

- **Total Recipe Cost: $3.53**
- **Hands-On Time:** 10 minutes
- **Cook Time:** 20 minutes

Serves 4

8 ounces frozen hash browns
6 precooked breakfast
   sausage patties
6 large eggs
¼ cup whole milk
½ teaspoon hot sauce
¼ teaspoon salt
⅛ teaspoon black pepper
½ cup shredded sharp
   Cheddar cheese
1½ cups water

1 Grease a 7" cake pan with cooking spray. Arrange frozen hash browns on the bottom of cake pan.

2 Place sausage patties in a single layer on top of hash browns with one in the center and five around edges.

3 In a small bowl, whisk together eggs, milk, hot sauce, salt, and pepper. Pour egg mixture over hash browns and sausage. Sprinkle cheese over top of hash brown casserole.

4 Place a paper towel on top of cake pan and tightly cover with foil.

5 Pour water into Instant Pot® and add trivet.

6 Create a foil sling with a long piece of foil folded lengthwise into thirds. Place it underneath cake pan. Use foil sling to gently lower pan into Instant Pot® so it sits on top of trivet. Fold foil sling over pan.

7 Close the lid and set pressure release to Sealing.

8 Press the Manual or Pressure Cook button and adjust the time to 20 minutes.

9 When the timer beeps, allow the pressure to release naturally for 5 minutes and then quick release the remaining pressure. Unlock lid and remove it.

10 Carefully remove the casserole using the foil sling. Remove the foil and paper towel from the top of the pan. Serve immediately.

PER SERVING

CALORIES: 499 | FAT: 36g | PROTEIN: 24g | SODIUM: 1,103mg
FIBER: 2g | CARBOHYDRATES: 19g | SUGAR: 2g

Sausage and Egg Sandwiches

In order to prevent water from getting into the eggs, it is important to tightly wrap each ramekin with foil, including the bottom.

- **Total Recipe Cost:** $4.10
- **Hands-On Time:** 10 minutes
- **Cook Time:** 9 minutes

Serves 4

4 large eggs
2 tablespoons whole milk
¼ teaspoon salt
⅛ teaspoon black pepper
1½ cups water
4 English muffins
2 teaspoons butter
4 breakfast sausage patties
4 slices Cheddar cheese

1 Spray four ramekins with cooking spray and set aside.

2 In a small bowl, whisk together eggs, milk, salt, and pepper. Pour evenly into four ramekins. Wrap ramekins tightly in foil.

3 Pour 1½ cups water into Instant Pot®.

4 Place foil-wrapped ramekins into Instant Pot®, stacked two by two. Close lid and set pressure release to Sealing.

5 Press Manual or Pressure Cook button and adjust time to 8 minutes.

6 While eggs are cooking, toast English muffins and spread with butter.

7 When the timer beeps, let pressure release naturally for 2 minutes and then quick release the remaining pressure. Unlock lid and remove it.

8 Carefully remove ramekins from Instant Pot®. Pour out water from cooking pot and put cooking pot back into Instant Pot®.

9 Press Sauté button and place sausage patties inside Instant Pot®. Heat sausage patties, turning once, 1 minute. Remove from Instant Pot®.

10 Remove each egg from its ramekin and place on one half of English muffin. Top each egg with a sausage patty and a slice of cheese. Place other half of the English muffin on top to create a sandwich.

PER SERVING

CALORIES: 454 | FAT: 27g | PROTEIN: 24g | SODIUM: 809mg
FIBER: 0g | CARBOHYDRATES: 28g | SUGAR: 1g

Cold Start Yogurt

This is a super creamy, lightly sweetened homemade yogurt recipe. Milk type is important for this recipe, so be sure to use the required ultra-pasteurized or ultra-filtered milk. You can keep 2 tablespoons of the yogurt in an air-tight container in the freezer. Thaw and use it in the next batch. If an unsweetened yogurt is desired, then omit the sweetened condensed milk.

- **Total Recipe Cost: $4.80**
- **Hands-On Time: 5 minutes**
- **Cook Time: 8 hours**

Serves 8

½ gallon ultra-pasteurized or ultra-filtered milk

7 ounces sweetened condensed milk

2 tablespoons plain yogurt with live active cultures

GREEK-STYLE YOGURT

Want to make super thick Greek-style yogurt? Follow the directions above and then strain the yogurt in a mesh strainer over a large bowl. Let the yogurt sit in the strainer in the refrigerator for 2–3 hours. The yogurt remaining in the mesh strainer is the Greek yogurt. The contents below in the bowl is the whey, which can be discarded or used in baked goods.

1 Start with a very clean Instant Pot® cooking pot.

2 In a medium bowl, whisk together milk, condensed milk, and yogurt.

3 Place lid on Instant Pot® (sealing ring can be removed) and press the Yogurt button. Set Instant Pot® to medium for 8 hours.

4 When the timer beeps, remove lid and refrigerate yogurt for a minimum of 8 hours.

5 Use within ten to fourteen days.

PER SERVING

CALORIES: 258 | FAT: 11g | PROTEIN: 10g | SODIUM: 149mg
FIBER: 0g | CARBOHYDRATES: 30g | SUGAR: 30g

Homemade Granola

This granola is made using the Instant Pot® slow cooker function. The trick to making crunchy granola in the Instant Pot® is by not fully covering the pot with a lid. Leaving some room for air flow will allow your granola to crisp up while cooking. It can be eaten as cereal with milk, as an easy snack on its own, or even over yogurt.

- **Total Recipe Cost:** $7.20
- **Hands-On Time:** 10 minutes
- **Cook Time:** 2 hours and 30 minutes

Serves 6

4 cups old-fashioned rolled oats

1 cup roasted almonds, roughly chopped

¼ cup packed light brown sugar

½ teaspoon ground cinnamon

½ teaspoon salt

½ cup olive oil

½ cup honey

1 teaspoon vanilla extract

½ cup dried cranberries

1 Spray inside of Instant Pot® with cooking spray.

2 Pour in rolled oats, almonds, brown sugar, cinnamon, and salt. Mix together.

3 In a small bowl, whisk together oil, honey, and vanilla.

4 Pour wet ingredients over dry ingredients in the pot and mix until fully combined.

5 Cover partially with a glass lid, leaving 3" of open air.

6 Press Slow Cook button and adjust time to 2½ hours. Let cook, stirring every 30 minutes.

7 When the timer beeps, remove lid and mix in cranberries. Remove granola from Instant Pot® and spread onto a large baking pan. Let cool.

8 Pour cooled granola into an air-tight container. Store at room temperature five to seven days.

PER SERVING

CALORIES: 753 | FAT: 35g | PROTEIN: 15g | SODIUM: 202mg
FIBER: 11g | CARBOHYDRATES: 100g | SUGAR: 43g

Chewy Chocolate Chip Granola Bars

These granola bars are an easy go-to breakfast or snack. They can be customized with whatever dried fruit or nuts you have on hand. The trick to getting them to stick together is to press them hard into the baking dish. If you spend a couple of minutes pressing them down, they are less likely to crumble up into granola.

- **Total Recipe Cost: $5.79**
- **Hands-On Time:** 10 minutes
- **Cook Time:** 5 minutes

Serves 8

1½ cups old-fashioned rolled oats
¼ cup packed light brown sugar
½ cup roasted whole almonds, chopped
¼ teaspoon salt
⅓ cup honey
¼ cup unsalted butter
1 teaspoon vanilla extract
½ cup dried cranberries
¾ cup mini chocolate chips, divided

1 Line an 8″ × 11″ baking pan with parchment paper and spray with cooking spray. Set aside.

2 In a medium bowl, mix together oats, brown sugar, almonds, and salt.

3 Turn Instant Pot® to Sauté. Place honey and butter into the Instant Pot® and allow them to melt together inside. Stir until mixture begins to bubble. Let bubble for 2 minutes; it will start to darken.

4 Turn Instant Pot® off and mix in vanilla.

5 Pour wet mixture over the dry mixture in the bowl and mix well.

6 Mix in cranberries. Mix in ½ cup chocolate chips. The chocolate chips will melt slightly, helping the bars to stick together.

7 Pour granola bar mixture into prepared baking pan. Use a spatula to firmly press granola bars into baking pan.

8 Pour remaining ¼ cup chocolate chips on top and press them into granola bars with a spatula. Refrigerate 2 hours.

9 Once chilled, cut into rectangles using a sharp knife. Store in an air-tight container, five to seven days.

PER SERVING

CALORIES: 362 | FAT: 17g | PROTEIN: 5g | SODIUM: 79mg
FIBER: 5g | CARBOHYDRATES: 53g | SUGAR: 35g

3

Soups

If you are new to making homemade soup, then you are in for a real treat! The recipes in this chapter taste so much better than their canned cousins. Homemade soup is an affordable way to eat at home, especially when you make your own broth to go with it.

Chicken Broth

Making Chicken Broth is very budget friendly because you can use scraps to make your own homemade broth for soups and recipes in the Instant Pot®. The recipe costs in this chapter are calculated using the cost of a store-bought broth. The recipes will cost even less if using homemade broth.

- **Total Recipe Cost: $2.35**
- **Hands-On Time: 5 minutes**
- **Cook Time: 30 minutes**

Yields 12 cups

Leftover bones and skin from 1 (4-pound) chicken

1 medium onion, peeled and roughly chopped

2 medium carrots, roughly chopped

2 medium stalks celery, roughly chopped

1 bay leaf

2 teaspoons salt

12 cups water

1 Place chicken bones and skin inside of Instant Pot®.

2 Place onion, carrots, and celery on top of chicken bones.

3 Add in bay leaf, salt, and water. Mix.

4 Close lid and set pressure release to Sealing.

5 Press Soup button and adjust time to 30 minutes.

6 When the timer beeps, allow pressure to release naturally and then unlock lid and remove it.

7 Strain Chicken Broth through a mesh strainer into a large bowl.

8 Ladle Chicken Broth into jars for refrigerator storage or freezer bags for freezer storage. Store in refrigerator up to one week or in freezer for up to three months.

PER SERVING (1 CUP)

CALORIES: 27 | FAT: 0g | PROTEIN: 4g | SODIUM: 477mg
FIBER: 1g | CARBOHYDRATES: 2g | SUGAR: 1g

Vegetable Broth

Making homemade Vegetable Broth is another great way to save money. Skins from onions and garlic along with any celery, onion, or carrot scraps can be saved in a bag in the freezer until it is time to make Vegetable Broth. Vegetable Broth may be used in place of Chicken Broth, as needed.

- **Total Recipe Cost: $1.75**
- **Hands-On Time: 5 minutes**
- **Cook Time: 30 minutes**

Yields 12 cups

- 2 medium stalks celery, roughly chopped
- 2 large carrots, roughly chopped
- 1 medium yellow onion, peeled and roughly chopped
- 4 cloves garlic, roughly chopped
- 1 tablespoon tomato paste
- 2 teaspoons salt
- ⅛ teaspoon black pepper
- 12 cups water

FREEZING CHICKEN AND VEGETABLE BROTH

Chicken and Vegetable Broth are both freezer friendly. Let it cool fully and then freeze in 2- or 4-cup portions using freezer-safe storage containers or zip-top freezer bags. If using freezer bags, lay the bag of broth sideways so it freezes flat. Once frozen, the broth can be stored in a small space in your freezer, leaving room for other items.

1. Place celery, carrots, onion, garlic, tomato paste, salt, and pepper in Instant Pot®.

2. Pour water into Instant Pot®. Mix until tomato paste is evenly distributed.

3. Close lid and set pressure release to Sealing.

4. Press Soup button and adjust time to 30 minutes.

5. When the timer beeps, allow pressure to release naturally and then unlock lid and remove it.

6. Strain Vegetable Broth through a mesh strainer into a large bowl.

7. Ladle Vegetable Broth into jars for refrigerator storage or freezer bags for freezer storage. Store in the refrigerator up to one week or in the freezer up to three months.

PER SERVING (1 CUP)

CALORIES: 12 | FAT: 0g | PROTEIN: 0g | SODIUM: 451mg
FIBER: 1g | CARBOHYDRATES: 3g | SUGAR: 3g

Loaded Baked Potato Soup

Loaded Baked Potato Soup in the Instant Pot® is a hearty and flavorful meal-sized soup. It's loaded with Yukon gold potatoes, bacon, half-and-half, and two different kinds of cheese.

- **Total Recipe Cost: $11.93**
- **Hands-On Time: 10 minutes**
- **Cook Time: 20 minutes**

Serves 6

4 thick-cut bacon slices cut into cubes

4 cups chicken broth

3 pounds Yukon gold potatoes, peeled

1 teaspoon salt

½ teaspoon black pepper

4 ounces cream cheese, melted

1 pint half-and-half

1 cup shredded sharp Cheddar cheese

2 medium green onions, sliced

1 Press Sauté button and cook bacon pieces in Instant Pot® until crisp. Press Cancel button.

2 Drain bacon fat and place cooked bacon in-between two paper towels. Set aside.

3 Pour in broth and deglaze pot.

4 Place whole potatoes, salt, and pepper into Instant Pot®. Close lid and set pressure release to Sealing.

5 Press Soup button and adjust time to 10 minutes.

6 When the timer beeps, quick release pressure, turn off Instant Pot®, and then unlock lid and remove it.

7 Using an immersion blender or potato masher, blend up potatoes and broth until only a few chunks are left.

8 Turn Instant Pot® back on and press Sauté button. Whisk in cream cheese and half-and-half. Let cook an additional 10 minutes, stirring occasionally.

9 Mix in half of the cooked bacon.

10 Serve topped with cheese, green onions, and remaining bacon.

PER SERVING

CALORIES: 578 | FAT: 36g | PROTEIN: 17g | SODIUM: 823mg
FIBER: 5g | CARBOHYDRATES: 49g | SUGAR: 6g

Beef Chili

Wow your friends and family with this hearty Instant Pot® Beef Chili recipe. Its robust flavor will make you come back for seconds!

- **Total Recipe Cost: $9.63**
- **Hands-On Time: 10 minutes**
- **Cook Time: 55 minutes**

Serves 6

1 tablespoon olive oil

1 medium yellow onion, peeled and diced

2 medium jalapeños, seeded and diced

2 pounds ground beef

1 teaspoon salt

1 teaspoon black pepper

3 cloves garlic, minced

2 (15-ounce) cans tomato sauce

2 (15.5-ounce) cans kidney beans, drained and rinsed

3 teaspoons chili powder

½ teaspoon cayenne pepper

¼ teaspoon red pepper flakes

1 Set Instant Pot® to Sauté. Add oil.

2 Pour in onion, jalapeños, and ground beef. Sprinkle with salt and pepper. Stir and cook until onions are soft and meat is no longer pink, about 8 minutes.

3 Add in garlic and cook an additional 30 seconds. Turn Instant Pot® off. Drain fat from the pot.

4 Mix in tomato sauce, kidney beans, chili powder, cayenne pepper, and red pepper flakes. Make sure to scrape the bottom of the pot for any stuck-on food.

5 Close lid and set pressure release to Sealing.

6 Press Bean/Chili button and set time to 45 minutes.

7 When the timer beeps, allow pressure to release naturally and then unlock lid and remove it. Serve.

PER SERVING

CALORIES: 502 | FAT: 26g | PROTEIN: 38g | SODIUM: 1,382mg
FIBER: 8g | CARBOHYDRATES: 29g | SUGAR: 6g

Tomato Basil Soup

Tomato Basil Soup is creamy and slightly spicy. It pairs well with crackers or a grilled cheese sandwich.

- **Total Recipe Cost: $7.90**
- **Hands-On Time: 5 minutes**
- **Cook Time: 9 minutes**

Serves 4

2 tablespoons olive oil
1 medium yellow onion, peeled and chopped
2 cloves garlic, minced
4 (14.5-ounce) cans diced tomatoes
2 cups vegetable broth
¼ cup fresh basil, chopped
2 tablespoons granulated sugar
1 teaspoon salt
1 cup heavy whipping cream

FRESH BASIL VERSUS DRIED BASIL

Dried basil is wonderful in many dishes, but there are some instances where fresh basil is required to carry the level of flavor needed. That is the case with this Tomato Basil Soup. If in a pinch, 2 tablespoons dried basil may be used in place of the ¼ cup fresh basil in this recipe. It will still be a great tomato soup but will not pack the same punch as the soup does when made with fresh basil.

1   Set Instant Pot® to Sauté. Put oil and onion into Instant Pot®. Cook onion 2 minutes until soft.

2   Add in garlic and cook 30 seconds. Turn Instant Pot® off.

3   Add tomatoes, vegetable broth, basil, sugar, and salt to Instant Pot® and stir to combine.

4   Close lid and set pressure release to Sealing.

5   Press Manual or Pressure Cook button and adjust time to 7 minutes.

6   When the timer beeps, quick release pressure and then unlock lid and remove it.

7   Blend soup with an immersion blender.

8   Once blended, whisk in heavy whipping cream and serve.

PER SERVING

CALORIES: 341 | FAT: 29g | PROTEIN: 4g | SODIUM: 822mg
FIBER: 3g | CARBOHYDRATES: 20g | SUGAR: 15g

Chicken Pot Pie Soup

Chicken pot pie in soup form is all of the delicious pot pie filling you love, and it's just hearty enough to be called a meal.

- **Total Recipe Cost:** $5.51
- **Hands-On Time:** 10 minutes
- **Cook Time:** 5 minutes

Serves 4

2 tablespoons olive oil

1 medium yellow onion, peeled and chopped

2 cloves garlic, minced

4 cups chicken broth

1 cup diced cooked chicken

1 (12-ounce) bag frozen mixed vegetables

2 teaspoons salt

½ teaspoon black pepper

½ teaspoon dried parsley

¼ teaspoon dried sage

1 bay leaf

1 cup heavy whipping cream

⅓ cup all-purpose flour

1 Set Instant Pot® to Sauté. Put oil and onion into Instant Pot®. Cook onion 2 minutes until soft.

2 Add in garlic and cook 30 seconds. Turn Instant Pot® off.

3 Add broth, chicken, mixed vegetables, salt, pepper, parsley, sage, and bay leaf.

4 Close lid and set pressure release to Sealing.

5 Press Manual or Pressure Cook button and adjust time to 2 minutes.

6 When the timer beeps, quick release pressure and then unlock lid and remove it.

7 In a small bowl, whisk together cream and flour. Whisk cream mixture into soup.

8 Remove bay leaf and serve.

PER SERVING

CALORIES: 472 | FAT: 31g | PROTEIN: 21g | SODIUM: 1,321mg
FIBER: 4g | CARBOHYDRATES: 29g | SUGAR: 8g

Cheesy Potato Soup

Warm up with a big batch of this Cheddar cheese potato soup. It's packed full of hearty red potatoes and creamy Cheddar cheese sauce!

- **Total Recipe Cost: $6.68**
- **Hands-On Time: 10 minutes**
- **Cook Time: 20 minutes**

Serves 8

3 pounds red potatoes, quartered

4 cups vegetable broth

4 cups water

2 teaspoons salt

½ teaspoon garlic powder

½ teaspoon onion powder

½ teaspoon dried oregano

¼ teaspoon black pepper

2 (15-ounce) cans Cheddar cheese sauce

1 Combine potatoes, broth, water, salt, garlic powder, onion powder, oregano, and pepper in Instant Pot®.

2 Close lid and set pressure release to Sealing.

3 Press Manual or Pressure Cook button and adjust time to 10 minutes.

4 When the timer beeps, quick release pressure and then unlock lid and remove it.

5 Blend soup using an immersion blender until smooth.

6 Press Sauté button and mix in Cheddar cheese sauce. Let cook, stirring occasionally, 10 minutes. Serve.

PER SERVING

CALORIES: 342 | **FAT:** 15g | **PROTEIN:** 14g | **SODIUM:** 968mg
FIBER: 4g | **CARBOHYDRATES:** 36g | **SUGAR:** 11g

Minestrone

This flavorful soup is packed with six different types of vegetables and two types of beans making it a hearty vegetarian soup.

- **Total Recipe Cost:** $5.81
- **Hands-On Time:** 10 minutes
- **Cook Time:** 13 minutes

Serves 6

2 tablespoons olive oil

1 medium yellow onion, peeled and chopped

2 cloves garlic, minced

4 cups vegetable broth

2 cups water

3 medium russet potatoes, peeled and cubed

2 medium carrots, diced

1 cup chopped green beans

2 teaspoons salt

1 teaspoon dried oregano

½ teaspoon black pepper

4 cups chopped kale

1 (15.5-ounce) can cannelloni beans, drained and rinsed

1 (15.5-ounce) can red kidney beans, drained and rinsed

½ cup medium shell-shaped pasta

1 Set Instant Pot® to Sauté. Put oil and onion into Instant Pot®. Cook onion 2 minutes until soft.

2 Add in garlic and cook 30 seconds. Turn Instant Pot® off.

3 Add broth, water, potatoes, carrots, green beans, salt, oregano, and pepper to Instant Pot® and mix.

4 Close lid and set pressure release to Sealing.

5 Press the Manual or Pressure Cook button and adjust time to 2 minutes.

6 When the timer beeps, quick release pressure and then unlock lid and remove it.

7 Press Sauté button. Mix in kale, cannelloni beans, kidney beans, and pasta. Let cook 8 minutes.

8 Turn Instant Pot® off and serve.

PER SERVING

CALORIES: 278 | FAT: 6g | PROTEIN: 11g | SODIUM: 1,044mg
FIBER: 9g | CARBOHYDRATES: 47g | SUGAR: 9g

Ham and Bean Soup

Ham and Bean Soup is a classic after-holiday recipe, using up leftover ham and bones. But it can be made any time with the use of a ham steak purchased from the grocery store. The cost of this soup is lower if using up leftover scraps that would have otherwise been discarded.

- **Total Recipe Cost:** $9.04
- **Hands-On Time:** 10 minutes
- **Cook Time:** 7 minutes

Serves 6

1 pound great northern beans
2 tablespoons olive oil
1 small yellow onion, peeled and chopped
6 cloves garlic, minced
1 (16-ounce) ham steak, cubed with bone reserved
6 cups chicken broth
2 medium carrots, diced
1 teaspoon dried parsley
½ teaspoon black pepper
1 bay leaf

NO SALT?

As you may notice, there isn't any salt listed in the ingredients list of this recipe. Ham contains a high salt content. Adding additional salt before tasting the cooked soup may result in an oversalted soup. Feel free to add salt after cooking, if needed.

1 Soak beans overnight or quick soak beans in Instant Pot®.

2 Set Instant Pot® to Sauté. Put oil and onion into Instant Pot®. Cook onion 2 minutes until soft.

3 Add in garlic and cook 30 seconds. Turn Instant Pot® off.

4 Add beans, ham and ham bone, broth, carrots, parsley, pepper, and bay leaf to Instant Pot®.

5 Close lid and set pressure release to Sealing.

6 Press Manual or Pressure Cook button and adjust time to 4 minutes.

7 When the timer beeps, quick release pressure and then unlock lid and remove it.

8 Remove bay leaf and ham bone. Serve.

PER SERVING

CALORIES: 435 | FAT: 9g | PROTEIN: 37g | SODIUM: 1,068mg
FIBER: 14g | CARBOHYDRATES: 53g | SUGAR: 5g

Pesto Tortellini Soup

Classic tortellini soup gets a twist thanks to the flavorful basil pesto served on top. This soup is ready in just a few quick minutes with the Instant Pot®.

- **Total Recipe Cost: $5.78**
- **Hands-On Time: 5 minutes**
- **Cook Time: 1 minute**

Serves 6

6 cups chicken broth

3 cups frozen tortellini

8 medium green onions, sliced

⅓ cup frozen chopped spinach

1½ teaspoons salt

¾ teaspoon black pepper

½ teaspoon dried oregano

½ cup basil pesto

1 Combine broth, tortellini, green onions, spinach, salt, pepper, and oregano in Instant Pot®.

2 Close lid and set pressure release to Sealing.

3 Press Manual or Pressure Cook button and adjust time to 1 minute.

4 When the timer beeps, quick release pressure and then unlock lid and remove it.

5 Ladle soup into bowls and top with pesto.

PER SERVING

CALORIES: 294 | FAT: 13g | PROTEIN: 14g | SODIUM: 1,105mg
FIBER: 4g | CARBOHYDRATES: 32g | SUGAR: 2g

New England Clam Chowder

Make creamy New England Clam Chowder with this easy Instant Pot® soup recipe. This affordable recipe tastes much better than the canned version.

- **Total Recipe Cost: $8.52**
- **Hands-On Time: 10 minutes**
- **Cook Time: 13 minutes**

Serves 4

2 tablespoons olive oil

1 medium yellow onion, peeled and chopped

3 cloves garlic, minced

1 cup chicken broth

3 small russet potatoes, peeled and cubed

1 (8-ounce) bottle clam juice

2 teaspoons salt

½ teaspoon black pepper

2 cups half-and-half

2 (6.5-ounce) cans minced clams

1 Set Instant Pot® to Sauté. Put oil and onion into Instant Pot®. Cook onion 2 minutes until soft.

2 Add in garlic and cook 30 seconds. Turn Instant Pot® off.

3 Add broth, potatoes, clam juice, salt, and pepper to Instant Pot®.

4 Close lid and set pressure release to Sealing.

5 Press Manual or Pressure Cook button and adjust time to 10 minutes.

6 When the timer beeps, quick release pressure and then unlock lid and remove it.

7 Whisk in half-and-half to the chowder. Mix in clams.

8 Serve.

PER SERVING

CALORIES: 420 | FAT: 30g | PROTEIN: 9g | SODIUM: 1,737mg
FIBER: 2g | CARBOHYDRATES: 31g | SUGAR: 6g

White Chicken Chili

White Chicken Chili is a tasty twist on traditional chili, using chicken breasts, white beans, and diced green chilies.

- **Total Recipe Cost:** $8.69
- **Hands-On Time:** 10 minutes
- **Cook Time:** 30 minutes

Serves 6

4 cups chicken broth

3 (14.5-ounce) cans cannellini beans

1 pound boneless, skinless chicken breasts

1 (16-ounce) can creamed corn

2 (4-ounce) cans mild diced green chilies

1 medium yellow onion, peeled and chopped

2 cloves garlic, minced

1 tablespoon chili powder

1 teaspoon salt

1 teaspoon dried oregano

½ teaspoon black pepper

½ teaspoon crushed red pepper

1 cup full-fat sour cream

1 Combine broth, beans, chicken, corn, green chilies, onion, garlic, chili powder, salt, oregano, black pepper, and crushed red pepper inside Instant Pot®.

2 Close lid and set pressure release to Sealing.

3 Press Manual or Pressure Cook button and adjust time to 30 minutes.

4 When the timer beeps, allow pressure to release naturally for 10 minutes and then quick release remaining pressure. Unlock lid and remove it.

5 Remove chicken from Instant Pot® and shred using two forks. Place chicken back into Instant Pot®. Mix in sour cream.

6 Serve hot.

PER SERVING

CALORIES: 403 | **FAT:** 10g | **PROTEIN:** 33g | **SODIUM:** 1,119mg
FIBER: 10g | **CARBOHYDRATES:** 49g | **SUGAR:** 13g

USING FROZEN CHICKEN IN WHITE CHICKEN CHILI

Frozen chicken breasts may be used in place of fresh chicken breasts in this recipe. The 30-minute cook time is enough time to fully cook the chicken, so no additional time is needed.

Sausage and Kale Soup

Sausage and Kale Soup feeds a crowd and is hearty enough to be eaten as a meal. If milder flavors are preferred, switch out the hot Italian sausage for mild Italian sausage.

- **Total Recipe Cost:** $9.38
- **Hands-On Time:** 10 minutes
- **Cook Time:** 18 minutes

Serves 8

1 tablespoon olive oil

1 pound hot Italian sausage, casings removed

4 cups chicken broth

4 cups water

6 medium russet potatoes, peeled and cubed

4 cups kale, stems removed

1 small yellow onion, peeled and chopped

3 cloves garlic, minced

½ teaspoon salt

⅛ teaspoon black pepper

1 cup heavy whipping cream

1 tablespoon flour

1 Set Instant Pot® to Sauté. Put oil and sausage into Instant Pot®. Cook sausage 8 minutes until brown, breaking it up into pieces while cooking. Turn Instant Pot® off.

2 Add broth, water, potatoes, kale, onion, garlic, salt, and pepper and stir to combine.

3 Close lid and set pressure release to Sealing.

4 Press Manual or Pressure Cook button and adjust time to 10 minutes.

5 When the timer beeps, quick release pressure and then unlock lid and remove it.

6 Whisk in heavy cream and flour. Serve.

PER SERVING

CALORIES: 350 | FAT: 21g | PROTEIN: 11g | SODIUM: 426mg
FIBER: 3g | CARBOHYDRATES: 31g | SUGAR: 3g

Broccoli Cheese Soup

This creamy and cheesy vegetable soup is made with fresh broccoli, carrots, and onion. Frozen broccoli may be used, but it should be defrosted and wrapped in a few paper towels to remove any excess water prior to cooking.

- **Total Recipe Cost: $11.25**
- **Hands-On Time: 15 minutes**
- **Cook Time: 13 minutes**

Serves 6

4 tablespoons unsalted butter

4 tablespoons all-purpose flour

4 cups chicken broth

2 medium bunches broccoli, stems removed

1 cup shredded carrots

1 cup chopped onion

1 teaspoon salt

¾ teaspoon black pepper

¼ teaspoon ground nutmeg

2 cups half-and-half

2 cups whole milk

3 cups shredded sharp Cheddar cheese

1 Set Instant Pot® to Sauté. Add butter and allow it to melt.

2 Once butter is melted, whisk in flour. Continue to whisk 3 minutes until the butter and flour are completely combined and the flour has turned golden brown.

3 Slowly whisk in broth.

4 Mix in broccoli, carrots, onion, salt, pepper, and nutmeg.

5 Close lid and set pressure release to Sealing.

6 Press Manual or Pressure Cook button and adjust time to 10 minutes.

7 When the timer beeps, allow pressure to release naturally for 10 minutes and then quick release remaining pressure. Unlock lid and remove it.

8 Whisk in half-and-half and milk. Blend soup with an immersion blender until smooth.

9 Fold in shredded cheese and mix until melted. Serve hot.

PER SERVING

CALORIES: 532 | FAT: 38g | PROTEIN: 25g | SODIUM: 946mg
FIBER: 4g | CARBOHYDRATES: 26g | SUGAR: 12g

Three Bean Chili

A simple meatless chili recipe that uses canned beans and is ready quickly.

- **Total Recipe Cost:** $7.90
- **Hands-On Time:** 5 minutes
- **Cook Time:** 16 minutes

Serves 4

2 tablespoons olive oil

1 medium yellow onion, peeled and chopped

1 medium green bell pepper, seeded and chopped

4 cloves garlic, minced

1 cup water

2 (15.5-ounce) cans red kidney beans, drained and rinsed

2 (15.5-ounce) cans black beans, drained and rinsed

2 (15.5-ounce) cans cannelloni beans, drained and rinsed

1 (15-ounce) can tomato sauce

1 (6-ounce) can tomato paste

1 tablespoon chili powder

1 teaspoon dried oregano

½ teaspoon cayenne pepper

1 Set Instant Pot® to Sauté. Add oil to pot. Add in onion and bell pepper and cook 5 minutes until soft.

2 Add in garlic and cook an additional 30 seconds until fragrant.

3 Pour in water and deglazed bottom of pot. Turn Instant Pot® off.

4 Add in kidney beans, black beans, cannelloni beans, tomato sauce, tomato paste, chili powder, oregano, and cayenne pepper. Mix well.

5 Close lid and set pressure release to Sealing.

6 Press Manual or Pressure Cook button and adjust time to 10 minutes.

7 When the timer beeps, quick release pressure and then unlock lid and remove it. Serve.

PER SERVING

CALORIES: 625 | FAT: 11g | PROTEIN: 36g | SODIUM: 1,355mg
FIBER: 28g | CARBOHYDRATES: 102g | SUGAR: 11g

Chicken and Dumplings

The dumplings in this dish are actually biscuits cut into small dumplings that cook on top of this creamy chicken soup.

- **Total Recipe Cost:** $8.73
- **Hands-On Time:** 10 minutes
- **Cook Time:** 16 minutes

Serves 6

1 cup all-purpose flour
2 teaspoons baking powder
1¼ teaspoons salt, divided
1½ cups whole milk, divided
6 tablespoons olive oil, divided
4 medium carrots, diced
2 pounds boneless, skinless chicken thighs, cut into 1" pieces
2 medium stalks celery, diced
1 medium yellow onion, peeled and diced
1½ cups sliced mushrooms
2 cloves garlic, minced
4 cups chicken broth
2 (10.5-ounce) cans cream of mushroom soup
½ teaspoon red pepper flakes
½ teaspoon black pepper

STORE-BOUGHT DUMPLINGS

One can of biscuit dough may be used in place of the dumplings and cut up as directed in the recipe. This is a great way to save a few minutes of prep time if you are in a hurry, but will increase the overall cost of the meal.

1 In a medium bowl, whisk together flour, baking powder, and 1 teaspoon salt.

2 Make a well in center of dry mixture and pour in ½ cup milk and 2 tablespoons olive oil.

3 Mix together with a fork until combined. This is your dumpling dough. Set aside.

4 Set Instant Pot® to Sauté. Pour in remaining 4 tablespoons olive oil.

5 Add in carrots, chicken, celery, onion, and mushrooms. Cover and cook 5 minutes until soft. Stir occasionally while it is cooking.

6 Remove lid and stir in minced garlic. Cook an additional 30 seconds.

7 Pour in chicken broth and deglaze pot.

8 Turn Instant Pot® off and whisk in cream of mushroom soup, remaining 1 cup milk, red pepper flakes, black pepper, and remaining ¼ teaspoon salt.

9 Rip dumpling dough into 1" pieces and toss on top of soup so they evenly cover top of the soup. A few might sink down.

10 Close lid and set pressure release to Sealing.

11 Press Manual or Pressure Cook button and adjust time to 10 minutes.

12 When the timer beeps, allow pressure to release naturally and then unlock lid and remove it. Serve.

PER SERVING

CALORIES: 529 | FAT: 24g | PROTEIN: 45g | SODIUM: 1,165mg
FIBER: 3g | CARBOHYDRATES: 34g | SUGAR: 9g

Chicken Tortilla Soup

This zesty soup recipe can be made with frozen chicken breasts. This saves time and allows it to be made at the last minute.

- **Total Recipe Cost:** $9.07
- **Hands-On Time:** 5 minutes
- **Cook Time:** 25 minutes

Serves 6

6 cups chicken broth

1 (6-ounce) can tomato paste

1 pound boneless, skinless chicken breasts

1 (15.25-ounce) can corn, drained

1 (14.5-ounce) can black beans, rinsed and drained

2 (7-ounce) cans mild diced green chilies

1 teaspoon salt

¼ teaspoon black pepper

2 cups tortilla chips

¼ cup cilantro, roughly chopped

1 Pour broth into Instant Pot®. Whisk tomato paste into broth.

2 Add in chicken breasts, corn, beans, green chilies, salt, and pepper. Stir to combine.

3 Close lid and set pressure release to Sealing.

4 Press Manual or Pressure Cook button and adjust time to 15 minutes.

5 When the timer beeps, allow pressure to release naturally for 10 minutes and then quick release remaining pressure. Unlock lid and remove it.

6 Remove chicken. Shred chicken using two forks and then place it back into Instant Pot®.

7 Serve soup topped with tortilla chips and cilantro.

PER SERVING

CALORIES: 289 | FAT: 6g | PROTEIN: 30g | SODIUM: 920mg
FIBER: 6g | CARBOHYDRATES: 32g | SUGAR: 10g

Potato Corn Chowder

This hearty soup is packed full of baby yellow potatoes, two different types of corn, onion, carrot, and celery, and is topped with flavorful bacon.

- **Total Recipe Cost: $8.73**
- **Hands-On Time: 15 minutes**
- **Cook Time: 20 minutes**

Serves 8

1 pound bacon, cut into ½" strips

2 medium stalks celery, diced

1 medium yellow onion, peeled and chopped

1 medium carrot, diced

2 cloves garlic, minced

4 cups vegetable broth

1½ pounds baby yellow potatoes, quartered

1 (15-ounce) can corn

1 (14.75-ounce) can creamed corn

2 teaspoons salt

¼ teaspoon black pepper

¼ teaspoon cayenne pepper

1 cup whole milk

4 medium green onions, sliced

1 Set Instant Pot® to Sauté. Add sliced bacon into Instant Pot®. Cook, stirring occasionally, for 7 minutes.

2 Remove bacon and place in between two paper towels. Set aside.

3 Remove bacon grease, reserving 2 tablespoons bacon grease inside Instant Pot®. Add celery, onion, and carrots. Cook, stirring occasionally, 7 minutes.

4 Add in garlic and cook an additional 30 seconds.

5 Pour in broth and deglaze the pot. Turn Instant Pot® off.

6 Mix in corn, creamed corn, salt, black pepper, and cayenne.

7 Close lid and set pressure release to Sealing.

8 Press Manual or Pressure Cook button and adjust time to 5 minutes.

9 When the timer beeps, quick release pressure and then unlock lid and remove it.

10 Slowly whisk in milk. Serve topped with cooked bacon and green onions.

PER SERVING

CALORIES: 392 | FAT: 24g | PROTEIN: 12g | SODIUM: 1,170mg
FIBER: 4g | CARBOHYDRATES: 33g | SUGAR: 9g

Beans, Rice, and Grains

Beans, rice, and grains are a staple in many frugal kitchens and for good reason. Not only are these kitchen staples extremely affordable but they freeze well and are very versatile. This chapter will show you how to make the basic staples and share several flavorful recipes. The Instant Pot® saves time thanks to its ability to "quick soak" beans in under an hour versus the traditional overnight method. The Instant Pot® also has built-in sensors that automatically set a time when using the Rice button.

White Rice

Whip up a batch of fluffy White Rice in just a few minutes, thanks to the Instant Pot®. This recipe can be doubled with the same cook time.

- **Total Recipe Cost: $0.40**
- **Hands-On Time: 5 minutes**
- **Cook Time: 12 minutes**

Yields 3 cups

1 cup dry white rice
1 cup water
⅛ teaspoon salt

WHITE RICE

White rice is the most versatile rice. It can take on the flavor of whatever herbs and spices you add to it. It also cooks quite quickly. The Rice button on the Instant Pot® will customize its cook time based on the weight of the water and rice added to the pot. You can rest assured that you will have moist and flavorful rice every time you make it in the Instant Pot®.

1 Place rice in a colander and rinse.

2 Combine rinsed rice, water, and salt in Instant Pot®.

3 Close lid and set pressure release to Sealing.

4 Press Rice button and adjust time to 12 minutes.

5 When the timer beeps, allow pressure to release naturally for 10 minutes and then quick release remaining pressure. Unlock lid and remove it.

6 Fluff rice with a fork and serve.

PER SERVING (1 CUP)

CALORIES: 225 | FAT: 0g | PROTEIN: 4g | SODIUM: 102mg
FIBER: 1g | CARBOHYDRATES: 49g | SUGAR: 0g

Brown Rice

This foolproof recipe makes cooking healthy Brown Rice easier than ever.

- **Total Recipe Cost:** $0.40
- **Hands-On Time:** 5 minutes
- **Cook Time:** 23 minutes

Yields 4 cups

1 cup dry brown rice
1 cup water
⅛ teaspoon salt

1 Place rice in a colander and rinse.

2 Combine rice, water, and salt in Instant Pot®.

3 Close lid and set pressure release to Sealing.

4 Press Multigrain button and adjust time to 23 minutes.

5 When the timer beeps, allow pressure to release naturally for 10 minutes and then quick release remaining pressure. Unlock lid and remove it.

6 Fluff rice with a fork and serve.

PER SERVING (1 CUP)

CALORIES: 172 | **FAT:** 1g | **PROTEIN:** 4g | **SODIUM:** 76mg
FIBER: 2g | **CARBOHYDRATES:** 36g | **SUGAR:** 0g

Wild Rice

If you are looking for a chewier and more flavorful rice, then consider making Wild Rice.

- **Total Recipe Cost:** $1.68
- **Hands-On Time:** 5 minutes
- **Cook Time:** 26 minutes

Yields 3 cups

1 cup dry wild rice
1 cup water
⅛ teaspoon salt

1 Place rice in a colander and rinse.

2 Combine rice, water, and salt in Instant Pot®.

3 Close lid and set pressure release to Sealing.

4 Press Multigrain button and adjust time to 26 minutes.

5 When the timer beeps, allow pressure to release naturally for 10 minutes and then quick release remaining pressure. Unlock lid and remove it.

6 Fluff rice with a fork and serve.

PER SERVING (1 CUP)

CALORIES: 190 | **FAT:** 1g | **PROTEIN:** 8g | **SODIUM:** 103mg
FIBER: 3g | **CARBOHYDRATES:** 40g | **SUGAR:** 1g

Vegetable Fried Rice

Have leftover cooked rice? Change up your leftovers with this Vegetable Fried Rice recipe. If you are going to reheat this recipe, remember to mix in 1 tablespoon water before reheating the leftovers.

- **Total Recipe Cost: $1.95**
- **Hands-On Time: 10 minutes**
- **Cook Time: 10 minutes**

Serves 4

2 tablespoons olive oil
½ medium white onion, peeled and chopped
1 medium carrot, diced
2 large eggs, lightly beaten
2 cups cooked white rice
1 cup frozen peas
2 tablespoons soy sauce

FRIED RICE

Fried rice can be customized based on your tastes and what you have on hand in your kitchen. The best way to save money on groceries is to use up what you already have and avoid going to the store for one or two missing ingredients. Instead, try substituting ingredients for what you have on hand. The oil in this recipe can easily be switched out for butter. The vegetables can be switched out for any vegetables you have on hand. Meat can also be added to make this more of a main dish.

1 Press Sauté button on Instant Pot®. Add oil and allow it to heat up.

2 Add onion and carrot to Instant Pot®. Cook until vegetables are soft, 5 minutes. Stir occasionally.

3 Move vegetables to side of pot and pour beaten eggs into empty spot in the Instant Pot®. Scramble eggs in the pot 3 minutes.

4 Pour in rice and peas. Stir and then cook an additional 2 minutes.

5 Mix in the soy sauce and turn Instant Pot® off.

6 Serve immediately.

PER SERVING

CALORIES: 250 | FAT: 10g | PROTEIN: 8g | SODIUM: 561mg
FIBER: 3g | CARBOHYDRATES: 33g | SUGAR: 3g

Spanish Rice

Spanish Rice is a zesty side dish that pairs nicely with Mexican food. The level of heat can be controlled by the type of salsa used.

- **Total Recipe Cost:** $3.30
- **Hands-On Time:** 10 minutes
- **Cook Time:** 9 minutes

Serves 6

2 tablespoons olive oil
1½ cups dry white rice
2 tablespoons diced onion
2 cups chicken broth
1 cup salsa

1 Push Sauté button and add oil. Add in rice and onion. Fry 5 minutes, stirring occasionally.

2 Pour broth into Instant Pot® and deglaze bottom of pot. Turn Instant Pot® off.

3 Add salsa and mix.

4 Close lid and set pressure release to Sealing.

5 Press Manual or Pressure Cook button and adjust time to 4 minutes.

6 When the timer beeps, allow pressure to release naturally for 10 minutes and then quick release remaining pressure. Unlock lid and remove it.

7 Fluff rice with a fork and serve.

PER SERVING

CALORIES: 231 | FAT: 5g | PROTEIN: 5g | SODIUM: 336mg
FIBER: 2g | CARBOHYDRATES: 41g | SUGAR: 2g

Cajun Dirty Rice

This recipe for Cajun Dirty Rice is a meatless version of the classic dish. It is called "dirty" rice because the onions, peppers, celery, and seasoning make the white rice a brownish color.

- **Total Recipe Cost: $2.94**
- **Hands-On Time:** 10 minutes
- **Cook Time:** 10 minutes

Serves 6

3 tablespoons olive oil

1½ cups dry white rice

1 medium stalk celery, chopped

½ medium yellow onion, peeled and chopped

½ medium green bell pepper, seeded and chopped

2 cloves garlic, minced

1 tablespoon Cajun seasoning

2 cups vegetable broth

1 Push Sauté button and add oil. Add in rice, celery, onion, and bell pepper and fry 5 minutes, stirring occasionally.

2 Add in garlic and cook an additional 30 seconds until fragrant. Season with Cajun seasoning.

3 Pour broth into Instant Pot® and deglaze bottom of pot. Turn Instant Pot® off.

4 Close lid and set pressure release to Sealing.

5 Press Manual or Pressure Cook button and adjust time to 4 minutes.

6 When the timer beeps, allow pressure to release naturally for 10 minutes and then quick release remaining pressure. Unlock lid and remove it.

7 Fluff rice with a fork and serve.

PER SERVING

CALORIES: 242 | FAT: 7g | PROTEIN: 4g | SODIUM: 95mg
FIBER: 1g | CARBOHYDRATES: 40g | SUGAR: 2g

Broccoli Cheese Rice

This pot-in-pot recipe is a great way to prepare a grain and vegetable at the same time and incorporate the two after they finish cooking.

- **Total Recipe Cost:** $4.69
- **Hands-On Time:** 10 minutes
- **Cook Time:** 9 minutes

Serves 6

2 tablespoons olive oil

1½ cups dry white rice

¼ teaspoon salt

¼ teaspoon black pepper

2 cups chicken broth

2 cups finely chopped broccoli

1 cup shredded sharp Cheddar cheese

1 tablespoon whole milk

1   Push Sauté button and add oil. Add in rice and fry 5 minutes, stirring occasionally.

2   Season with salt and pepper. Pour broth into Instant Pot® and deglaze bottom of pot.

3   Turn Instant Pot® off. Place a trivet inside the Instant Pot® with a steamer basket on top.

4   Add broccoli to steamer basket.

5   Close lid and set pressure release to Sealing.

6   Press Manual or Pressure Cook button and adjust time to 4 minutes.

7   When the timer beeps, allow pressure to release naturally for 10 minutes and then quick release remaining pressure. Unlock lid and remove it.

8   Remove steamer basket with broccoli, and trivet.

9   Mix broccoli, cheese, and milk into rice. Serve.

PER SERVING

CALORIES: 306 | **FAT:** 11g | **PROTEIN:** 10g | **SODIUM:** 263mg **FIBER:** 2g | **CARBOHYDRATES:** 40g | **SUGAR:** 1g

Chicken Herb Rice

Chicken Herb Rice tastes just like the boxed variety famously known as "The San Francisco Treat." This recipe makes heaping servings for just a couple of dollars.

- **Total Recipe Cost: $2.89**
- **Hands-On Time:** 10 minutes
- **Cook Time:** 9 minutes

Serves 6

2 tablespoons olive oil

1½ cups dry white rice

1 medium yellow onion, peeled and diced

1 tablespoon dried parsley

1 teaspoon granulated sugar

½ teaspoon celery seed

¼ teaspoon salt

2 cups chicken broth

FREEZING RICE

Rice can easily be frozen. It is important to make sure the rice is fully cooled before freezing. You will want to freeze rice in either air-tight containers or zip-top freezer bags. Most rice dishes will stay fresh up to three months in the freezer. When ready to use, defrost the dish overnight in the refrigerator. Then you can reheat it either on the stovetop or in the microwave or oven. Just mix in a little bit of water or broth to prevent the rice from drying out.

1   Push Sauté button and add oil. Add in rice and onion and fry 5 minutes, stirring occasionally.

2   Season with parsley, sugar, celery seed, and salt. Stir to combine.

3   Pour broth into Instant Pot® and deglaze bottom of pot. Turn Instant Pot® off.

4   Close lid and set pressure release to Sealing.

5   Press Manual or Pressure Cook button and adjust time to 4 minutes.

6   When the timer beeps, allow pressure to release naturally for 10 minutes and then quick release remaining pressure. Unlock lid and remove it.

7   Fluff rice with a fork and serve.

PER SERVING

CALORIES: 229 | FAT: 5g | PROTEIN: 5g | SODIUM: 131mg
FIBER: 1g | CARBOHYDRATES: 40g | SUGAR: 2g

Rice Pilaf

Rice Pilaf is a nice change from the traditional rice dishes. It is a combination of white rice and orzo pasta, cooked together in the same dish along with chicken broth, garlic, and onion.

- **Total Recipe Cost: $2.22**
- **Hands-On Time:** 10 minutes
- **Cook Time:** 10 minutes

Serves 4

2 tablespoons olive oil
1 cup dry white rice
½ medium onion, peeled and diced
2 cloves garlic, minced
¼ teaspoon salt
⅛ teaspoon black pepper
2 cups chicken broth
½ cup orzo pasta

1 Push Sauté button and add oil. Add in rice and onion and fry 5 minutes, stirring occasionally.

2 Add in garlic, salt, and pepper. Cook an additional 30 seconds.

3 Pour broth into Instant Pot® and deglaze bottom of pot. Turn Instant Pot® off. Mix in pasta.

4 Close lid and set pressure release to Sealing.

5 Press Manual or Pressure Cook button and adjust time to 4 minutes.

6 When the timer beeps, allow pressure to release naturally for 10 minutes and then quick release remaining pressure. Unlock lid and remove it.

7 Fluff pilaf with a fork and serve.

PER SERVING

CALORIES: 342 | FAT: 8g | PROTEIN: 9g | SODIUM: 194mg
FIBER: 2g | CARBOHYDRATES: 58g | SUGAR: 2g

Spicy Mushroom Rice

As the name states, this is a spicier rice. It's made with fresh mushrooms and fresh jalapeños. If you want to strengthen the heat, leave the seeds inside of the jalapeño.

- **Total Recipe Cost: $4.61**
- **Hands-On Time: 10 minutes**
- **Cook Time: 10 minutes**

Serves 6

3 tablespoons olive oil
1½ cups dry white rice
1 cup sliced mushrooms
1 medium shallot, peeled and diced
1 medium jalapeño, seeded and diced
½ teaspoon black pepper
½ teaspoon crushed red pepper flakes
¼ teaspoon salt
2 cups chicken broth

1 Push Sauté button and add oil. Add in rice, mushrooms, shallot, jalapeño, black pepper, red pepper, and salt. Fry 5 minutes, stirring occasionally.

2 Pour broth into Instant Pot® and deglaze bottom of pot. Turn Instant Pot® off.

3 Close lid and set pressure release to Sealing.

4 Press Manual or Pressure Cook button and adjust time to 4 minutes.

5 When the timer beeps, allow pressure to release naturally for 10 minutes and then quick release remaining pressure. Unlock lid and remove it.

6 Fluff rice with a fork and serve.

PER SERVING

CALORIES: 246 | FAT: 7g | PROTEIN: 5g | SODIUM: 228mg
FIBER: 1g | CARBOHYDRATES: 39g | SUGAR: 1g

Quick Soaked Beans

The Instant Pot® makes quick work of dried beans. Instead of having to soak your beans overnight, they can be quick soaked in the Instant Pot® and ready for your favorite recipe in under an hour. Any variety of dried beans will work with this quick soak method. Use these beans in place of canned beans in recipes or in recipes requiring soaked beans.

- **Total Recipe Cost: $0.92**
- **Hands-On Time:** 10 minutes
- **Cook Time:** 5 minutes

Yields 6 cups

1 pound (2 cups) dried beans
Water to cover beans

WHY BEANS?

Beans are a great thing to keep on hand because they are affordable. Dried beans can be stored at room temperature for one to two years. One pound of beans can be purchased for under $2 in most areas. In addition to being affordable, beans are a great source of protein, fiber, and many vitamins. Most are also low in fat.

1 Rinse dried beans in a colander and pick out and dispose of any stones.

2 Pour rinsed beans into Instant Pot®. Fill pot with water until water is 1″ above top of beans.

3 Close lid and set pressure release to Sealing.

4 Press Manual or Pressure Cook button and adjust time to 5 minutes.

5 When the timer beeps, allow pressure to release naturally, then unlock lid, remove it, and drain out any access water.

6 Store any unused beans in an air-tight container in the refrigerate up to seven days or in the freezer up to three months.

PER SERVING (1 CUP)

CALORIES: 252 | FAT: 1g | PROTEIN: 18g | SODIUM: 18mg
FIBER: 19g | CARBOHYDRATES: 45g | SUGAR: 2g

Simple Seasoned Black Beans

A simple black bean recipe that does not require presoaking. Serve these simple seasoned black beans along with Spanish Rice (see recipe in this chapter) or your favorite Mexican dish.

- **Total Recipe Cost: $3.81**
- **Hands-On Time: 5 minutes**
- **Cook Time: 25 minutes**

Serves 8

6 cups vegetable broth
1 pound black beans
1 tablespoon onion powder
1 teaspoon dried oregano
¼ teaspoon salt
¼ teaspoon garlic powder
⅛ teaspoon black pepper

1 Combine all ingredients in Instant Pot®.

2 Close lid and set pressure release to Sealing.

3 Press Manual or Pressure Cook button and adjust time to 25 minutes.

4 When the timer beeps, allow pressure to release naturally and then unlock lid and remove it.

5 Serve.

PER SERVING

CALORIES: 205 | FAT: 1g | PROTEIN: 12g | SODIUM: 126mg
FIBER: 10g | CARBOHYDRATES: 39g | SUGAR: 3g

Cheesy Black Beans

Cheesy Black Beans are a flavorful black bean side dish, made extra special thanks to the Cheddar cheese topping.

- **Total Recipe Cost: $7.42**
- **Hands-On Time: 10 minutes**
- **Cook Time: 31 minutes**

Serves 8

2 tablespoons olive oil

½ medium yellow onion, peeled and diced

2 cloves garlic, minced

6 cups vegetable broth

1 pound dry black beans

1 (4-ounce) can mild diced green chilies

1 bay leaf

1 teaspoon cumin

1 teaspoon dried oregano

¼ teaspoon salt

⅛ teaspoon black pepper

2 cups shredded sharp Cheddar cheese

1 Push Sauté button and add oil. Add in onion and fry 5 minutes, stirring occasionally.

2 Add in garlic and cook an additional 30 seconds.

3 Pour broth into Instant Pot® and deglaze bottom of pot. Turn Instant Pot® off.

4 Mix in beans, diced green chilies, bay leaf, cumin, oregano, salt, and pepper.

5 Close lid and set pressure release to Sealing.

6 Press Manual or Pressure Cook button and adjust time to 25 minutes.

7 When the timer beeps, allow pressure to release naturally and then unlock lid and remove it.

8 Stir in cheese. Serve once the cheese is melted.

PER SERVING

CALORIES: 353 | FAT: 14g | PROTEIN: 19g | SODIUM: 351mg
FIBER: 10g | CARBOHYDRATES: 41g | SUGAR: 4g

Refried Beans

You can't beat homemade refried beans. Not only do they taste great, but they cost so much less than the price per can of refried beans. They can be ready in just over an hour—start to finish—thanks to the Instant Pot®.

- **Total Recipe Cost:** $6.34
- **Hands-On Time:** 10 minutes
- **Cook Time:** 51 minutes

Serves 8

2 tablespoons olive oil

1 medium yellow onion, peeled and chopped

3 cloves garlic, minced

7 cups chicken broth

1 pound dry pinto beans

1 (7-ounce) can mild diced green chilies

1 teaspoon cumin

½ teaspoon black pepper

¼ teaspoon salt

⅛ teaspoon cayenne pepper

REFRIED BEANS

Refried beans are a staple in many Mexican cuisines. They can be served as a side dish or mixed into dishes such as burritos, tacos, and enchiladas. To freeze refried beans, start by letting them fully cool. Then, separate them into 1- to 2-cup freezer-safe containers. Label and freeze them up to three months. They may be defrosted at room temperature or overnight in the refrigerator.

1 Push Sauté button and add oil. Add in onion and fry 5 minutes, stirring occasionally.

2 Add in garlic and cook an additional 30 seconds.

3 Pour broth into Instant Pot® and deglaze bottom of pot. Turn Instant Pot® off.

4 Mix in beans, green chilies, cumin, black pepper, salt, and cayenne pepper.

5 Close lid and set pressure release to Sealing.

6 Press Manual or Pressure Cook button and adjust time to 45 minutes.

7 When the timer beeps, allow pressure to release naturally and then unlock lid and remove it.

8 Drain beans through a mesh sieve. Reserve 2 cups liquid.

9 Place cooked beans and 2 cups liquid back into Instant Pot®. Blend beans using an immersion blender. Serve.

PER SERVING

CALORIES: 240 | FAT: 4g | PROTEIN: 13g | SODIUM: 150mg
FIBER: 9g | CARBOHYDRATES: 38g | SUGAR: 3g

"Baked" Beans

Make this classic "Baked" Beans recipe in no time using the Instant Pot®. Simply quick soak a pound of beans, fry up some bacon, and you will have a delicious pot of "Baked" Beans ready to enjoy at your next barbecue.

- **Total Recipe Cost:** $7.98
- **Hands-On Time:** 10 minutes
- **Cook Time:** 25 minutes

Serves 8

1 pound bacon,
    sliced into 1" pieces
1 medium yellow onion,
    peeled and diced
1 medium red bell pepper,
    seeded and diced
1 cup water
2 cups dried navy beans,
    soaked
1 cup ketchup
1 cup brown sugar
2 tablespoons
    Worcestershire sauce

1. Push Sauté button on Instant Pot®. Spray inside of Instant Pot® with cooking spray and place in bacon slices. Let cook 7 minutes until bacon is browned, stirring occasionally.

2. Remove bacon and place in between two paper towels to drain grease.

3. Dispose of bacon grease, reserving 2 tablespoons inside the Instant Pot®. Add onion and bell pepper into remaining bacon grease. Let cook 3 minutes until soft, stirring occasionally.

4. Pour in water and deglaze the bottom of the pot. Turn Instant Pot® off.

5. Add in soaked beans, ketchup, brown sugar, and Worcestershire. Stir to combine.

6. Close lid and set pressure release to Sealing.

7. Press Manual or Pressure Cook button and adjust time to 15 minutes.

8. When the timer beeps, allow pressure to release naturally, and then unlock lid and remove it.

9. Serve warm and refrigerate any leftovers up to one week.

PER SERVING

CALORIES: 564 | FAT: 23g | PROTEIN: 19g | SODIUM: 737mg
FIBER: 9g | CARBOHYDRATES: 72g | SUGAR: 38g

White Beans with Rosemary and Garlic

This simple white bean recipe gains its flavor from fresh herbs and flavor-packed garlic and onion powder. In a pinch, you can use dried rosemary but it won't have quite as much flavor as the fresh rosemary.

- **Total Recipe Cost:** $5.99
- **Hands-On Time:** 10 minutes
- **Cook Time:** 30 minutes

Serves 8

1 pound dry navy beans
6 cups vegetable broth
6 springs fresh rosemary
1 tablespoon onion powder
2 teaspoons garlic powder
½ teaspoon salt
1 bay leaf

1 Combine all ingredients in Instant Pot®. Close lid and set pressure release to Sealing.

2 Press Manual or Pressure Cook button and adjust time to 30 minutes.

3 When the timer beeps, allow pressure to release naturally and then unlock lid and remove it.

4 Serve.

PER SERVING

CALORIES: 207 | FAT: 1g | PROTEIN: 13g | SODIUM: 197mg
FIBER: 10g | CARBOHYDRATES: 38g | SUGAR: 4g

Restaurant-Style Pinto Beans

Like refried beans, pinto beans are a staple at many Mexican restaurants. These pinto beans are cooked with an array of spices, giving them that zesty flavor you get at your favorite restaurant.

- **Total Recipe Cost:** $4.62
- **Hands-On Time:** 10 minutes
- **Cook Time:** 51 minutes

Serves 8

2 tablespoons olive oil

1 medium yellow onion, peeled and diced

4 cloves garlic, minced

4 cups chicken broth

1 pound dry pinto beans

2 tablespoons chili powder

1 teaspoon cumin

1 teaspoon dried oregano

½ teaspoon salt

¼ teaspoon black pepper

1 Push Sauté button and add oil. Add in onion and fry 5 minutes, stirring occasionally.

2 Add in garlic and cook an additional 30 seconds.

3 Pour broth into Instant Pot® and deglaze bottom of pot. Turn Instant Pot® off.

4 Mix in beans, chili powder, cumin, oregano, salt, and pepper.

5 Close lid and set pressure release to Sealing.

6 Press Manual or Pressure Cook button and adjust time to 45 minutes.

7 When the timer beeps, allow pressure to release naturally and then unlock lid and remove it. Serve.

PER SERVING

CALORIES: 253 | FAT: 5g | PROTEIN: 15g | SODIUM: 256mg
FIBER: 10g | CARBOHYDRATES: 39g | SUGAR: 2g

Appetizers and Sauces

The Instant Pot® really shines when it comes to making appetizers. It allows you to whip up something delicious with very little hands-on time. Now you can focus more time on entertaining your friends and family. In this chapter, you will find tasty dips like Artichoke Dip and Nacho Cheese Dip along with crave-worthy meatball and chicken wing recipes. We also show you how to make your own homemade Alfredo Sauce!

Artichoke Dip

This cheesy Artichoke Dip is made with just a handful of ingredients. This recipe is very hands-off and cooks in just 7 minutes. It's best to make this recipe on the same day you plan to serve it and dish it up hot. Serve this dip with chips or celery.

- **Total Recipe Cost: $6.98**
- **Hands-On Time: 5 minutes**
- **Cook Time: 7 minutes**

Serves 6

1 (13.75-ounce) can quartered artichoke hearts, drained

1 (7-ounce) can mild diced green chilies

1 cup mayonnaise

1 teaspoon paprika

½ teaspoon garlic powder

2 cups shredded mozzarella cheese

1 cup grated Parmesan cheese

1 Combine artichoke hearts, green chilies, mayonnaise, paprika, and garlic powder in Instant Pot®.

2 Close lid and set pressure release to Sealing.

3 Press Manual or Pressure Cook button and adjust time to 7 minutes.

4 When the timer beeps, quick release pressure and then unlock lid and remove it.

5 Mix in cheeses and serve hot.

PER SERVING

CALORIES: 434 | FAT: 40g | PROTEIN: 15g | SODIUM: 793mg
FIBER: 0g | CARBOHYDRATES: 4g | SUGAR: 1g

SPINACH ARTICHOKE DIP
If you would rather make Spinach Artichoke Dip, mix in 6 ounces of frozen chopped spinach before cooking in the Instant Pot®.

Nacho Cheese Dip

This easy cheese dip is made using the Sauté function of the Instant Pot®. It is important to not walk away while making this dip as it can easily burn if left unattended.

- **Total Recipe Cost:** $5.10
- **Hands-On Time:** 5 minutes
- **Cook Time:** 14 minutes

Serves 8

2 tablespoons unsalted butter

2 tablespoons all-purpose flour

1 cup whole milk

1 teaspoon hot sauce

4 cups shredded sharp Cheddar cheese

1 (10-ounce) can diced tomatoes with green chilies

1 Push Sauté button and melt butter.

2 Whisk in flour and stir constantly 3 minutes until flour is combined with butter and golden brown.

3 Slowly whisk in milk. Continue mixing 3 minutes until sauce is no longer lumpy. Mix in hot sauce.

4 Add in cheese 1 cup at a time and stir 5 minutes until fully melted.

5 Fold in diced tomatoes. Let cook 3 minutes, stirring occasionally, until hot.

6 Press Keep Warm button and serve directly from Instant Pot®.

PER SERVING

CALORIES: 288 | FAT: 23g | PROTEIN: 14g | SODIUM: 527mg
FIBER: 0g | CARBOHYDRATES: 6g | SUGAR: 3g

Honey Barbecue Meatballs

These sweet and savory meatballs coated in a sticky barbecue sauce are sure to become a family favorite.

- **Total Recipe Cost:** $4.89
- **Hands-On Time:** 10 minutes
- **Cook Time:** 10 minutes

Serves 6

1 pound ground beef
1 large egg
½ cup bread crumbs
1 teaspoon minced onion
¼ teaspoon garlic powder
¼ teaspoon salt
⅛ teaspoon black pepper
2 tablespoons olive oil
1 cup water
1 cup barbecue sauce
½ cup honey
2 tablespoons brown sugar

1 In a medium bowl, combine ground beef, egg, bread crumbs, onion, garlic powder, salt, and pepper. Use clean hands to mix until fully combined, about 3 minutes.

2 Roll beef mixture into golf ball–sized meatballs.

3 Press Sauté button on Instant Pot® and add oil.

4 Working in batches, brown meatballs in Instant Pot® until golden brown on the outside, 1 minute on each side. Remove meatballs and set aside.

5 Pour water into Instant Pot® and deglaze the pot. Turn Instant Pot® off. Place meatballs inside Instant Pot®.

6 In a small bowl, whisk together barbecue sauce, honey, and brown sugar. Pour sauce over meatballs and turn to coat.

7 Close lid and set pressure release to Sealing.

8 Press Manual or Pressure Cook button and adjust time to 4 minutes.

9 When the timer beeps, allow pressure to release manually and then unlock lid and remove it. Serve meatballs on toothpicks.

PER SERVING

CALORIES: 431 | **FAT:** 17g | **PROTEIN:** 17g | **SODIUM:** 693mg
FIBER: 1g | **CARBOHYDRATES:** 53g | **SUGAR:** 43g

Teriyaki Meatballs

Teriyaki Meatballs are an easy and tasty cocktail meatball, made with ground beef, carrots, and green onions. Then they are cooked directly in teriyaki sauce, making them moist and flavorful.

- **Total Recipe Cost:** $5.19
- **Hands-On Time:** 10 minutes
- **Cook Time:** 10 minutes

Serves 6

1 pound ground beef
1 large egg
½ cup bread crumbs
¼ cup diced green onions
¼ cup shredded carrots
1 clove garlic, minced
2 tablespoons olive oil
1½ cups teriyaki sauce

1 In a medium bowl, combine ground beef, egg, bread crumbs, green onions, carrots, and garlic. Use clean hands to mix until fully combined, about 3 minutes.

2 Roll beef mixture into golf ball–sized meatballs.

3 Press Sauté button on Instant Pot® and add oil.

4 Working in batches, brown meatballs in Instant Pot® until golden brown on the outside, 1 minute on each side. Remove meatballs and set aside.

5 Pour teriyaki sauce into Instant Pot® and deglaze the pot. Turn Instant Pot® off.

6 Place meatballs inside Instant Pot® and turn to coat in sauce.

7 Close lid and set pressure release to Sealing.

8 Press Manual or Pressure Cook button and adjust time to 4 minutes.

9 When the timer beeps, allow pressure to release manually and then unlock lid and remove it. Serve meatballs on toothpicks.

PER SERVING

CALORIES: 318 | FAT: 17g | PROTEIN: 21g | SODIUM: 2,891mg
FIBER: 1g | CARBOHYDRATES: 19g | SUGAR: 11g

Buffalo Chicken Meatballs

Like a buffalo wing in meatball form, these Buffalo Chicken Meatballs are slightly spicy with blue cheese mixed in. Add more sauce if you want a spicier meatball. Ground chicken is pretty common in most grocery stores these days, but if you can't find it, just throw a pound of boneless skinless chicken breasts in a food processor to grind.

- **Total Recipe Cost: $7.06**
- **Hands-On Time: 10 minutes**
- **Cook Time: 20 minutes**

Serves 6

1 pound ground chicken
1 large egg
½ cup bread crumbs
1 cup shredded carrots
⅛ cup minced green onions
¼ cup minced celery
2 cloves garlic, minced
2 ounces blue cheese crumbles
2 tablespoons olive oil
½ cup water
1 cup buffalo sauce

1 In a medium bowl, combine chicken, egg, bread crumbs, carrots, green onions, celery, garlic, and blue cheese. Use clean hands to mix until fully combined, about 3 minutes.

2 Roll chicken mixture into golf ball–sized meatballs.

3 Press Sauté button on Instant Pot® and add oil.

4 Working in batches, brown meatballs in Instant Pot® until golden brown on the outside, 1 minute on each side. Remove meatballs and set aside.

5 Pour water into Instant Pot® and deglaze the pot. Turn Instant Pot® off.

6 Place meatballs inside Instant Pot® and pour buffalo sauce on top. Turn meatballs to coat in sauce.

7 Close lid and set pressure release to Sealing.

8 Press Manual or Pressure Cook button and adjust time to 15 minutes.

9 When the timer beeps, allow pressure to release manually and then unlock lid and remove it. Serve meatballs on toothpicks with drizzled sauce from pot.

PER SERVING

CALORIES: 290 | FAT: 11g | PROTEIN: 22g | SODIUM: 647mg
FIBER: 1g | CARBOHYDRATES: 25g | SUGAR: 15g

Classic Deviled Eggs

Deviled eggs are a party staple and very affordable to make. It doesn't take a lot of ingredients to make these delicious eggs and chances are you might have all the ingredients on hand already, making them perfect if you need to whip up a last-minute appetizer.

- **Total Recipe Cost:** $1.42
- **Hands-On Time:** 15 minutes
- **Cook Time:** 5 minutes

Serves 4

1½ cups water
6 large eggs
⅛ cup mayonnaise
⅛ cup mustard
1 teaspoon white vinegar
⅛ teaspoon salt
⅛ teaspoon black pepper
¼ teaspoon paprika

1 Pour water into Instant Pot®. Place a trivet inside Instant Pot® and arrange eggs on top of trivet.

2 Close lid and set pressure release to Sealing.

3 Press Manual or Pressure Cook button and adjust time to 5 minutes.

4 When the timer beeps, allow pressure to release naturally for 5 minutes and then quick release remaining pressure. Unlock lid and remove it.

5 Carefully place eggs into a bowl of ice water. Leave eggs in ice bath 5 minutes. Remove eggs and peel.

6 Slice eggs in half and carefully scoop out yolk with a spoon. Place all yolks in a small bowl.

7 Add mayonnaise, mustard, vinegar, salt, and pepper to bowl of yolks. Mix until fully combined.

8 Scoop heaping spoonfuls of egg yolk mixture into center of halved hard-boiled eggs.

9 Sprinkle paprika on top of each deviled egg.

10 Chill eggs up to 24 hours until ready to be served.

PER SERVING

CALORIES: 159 | FAT: 13g | PROTEIN: 10g | SODIUM: 306mg
FIBER: 0g | CARBOHYDRATES: 1g | SUGAR: 0g

Ranch Deviled Eggs

Ranch Deviled Eggs are a milder version of Classic Deviled Eggs (see recipe in this chapter) with the flavors of parsley, dill, and basil mixed right in.

- **Total Recipe Cost:** $1.67
- **Hands-On Time:** 15 minutes
- **Cook Time:** 5 minutes

Serves 4

1½ cups water
6 large eggs
⅛ cup mayonnaise
⅛ cup full-fat sour cream
1 teaspoon white vinegar
¼ teaspoon dried parsley
¼ teaspoon dill weed
⅛ teaspoon salt
⅛ teaspoon garlic powder
⅛ teaspoon onion powder
⅛ teaspoon dried basil

SPICE PRICES

If you don't have the spices on hand for this recipe, then this recipe may end up being more expensive than what was listed to account for your having to purchase a container of each spice. Instead, try buying a ranch seasoning packet at your grocery store to use in place of the spices listed.

1 Pour water into Instant Pot®.

2 Place a trivet inside Instant Pot® and arrange eggs on top of trivet.

3 Close lid and set pressure release to Sealing.

4 Press Manual or Pressure Cook button and adjust time to 5 minutes.

5 When the timer beeps, allow pressure to release naturally for 5 minutes and then quick release remaining pressure. Unlock lid and remove it.

6 Carefully place eggs into a bowl of ice water. Leave eggs in ice bath 5 minutes. Remove eggs and peel.

7 Slice eggs in half and carefully scoop out yolk with a spoon. Place all yolks in a small bowl.

8 Add mayonnaise, sour cream, vinegar, parsley, dill weed, salt, garlic powder, onion powder, and basil to bowl of yolks. Mix until fully combined.

9 Scoop heaping spoonfuls of egg yolk mixture into center of halved hard-boiled eggs.

10 Chill eggs up to 24 hours until ready to be served.

PER SERVING

CALORIES: 167 | **FAT:** 13g | **PROTEIN:** 10g | **SODIUM:** 225mg
FIBER: 0g | **CARBOHYDRATES:** 1g | **SUGAR:** 1g

Buffalo Wings

Buffalo Wings are so easy to make in the Instant Pot®. They cook quickly and the meat comes out fall-off-the-bone tender. This recipe calls for frozen chicken wings. If using fresh or thawed wings, cut the cook time down to 10 minutes.

- **Total Recipe Cost: $6.35**
- **Hands-On Time: 10 minutes**
- **Cook Time: 15 minutes**

Serves 4

2 pounds frozen chicken wings
½ tablespoon Cajun seasoning
1½ cups water
1 cup buffalo wing sauce

WANT CRISPIER WINGS?

If you want crispier wings, spread them out on a foil-lined baking pan and crisp them under the boiler of your oven for 4 minutes on each side.

1 In a large bowl, toss chicken wings in Cajun seasoning so they are evenly coated.

2 Pour water into Instant Pot® and add a trivet.

3 Place wings in a 7" springform pan. Create a foil sling and lower pan into Instant Pot®.

4 Close lid and set pressure release to Sealing.

5 Press Manual or Pressure Cook button and adjust time to 15 minutes.

6 When the timer beeps, allow pressure to release naturally and then unlock lid and remove it. Remove pan from Instant Pot® using foil sling.

7 Remove wings and brush with buffalo sauce. Serve hot.

PER SERVING

CALORIES: 337 | FAT: 16g | PROTEIN: 22g | SODIUM: 768mg
FIBER: 1g | CARBOHYDRATES: 24g | SUGAR: 20g

Barbecue Wings

Barbecue Wings are a tasty spin on the classic Buffalo Wing recipe. These wings are sweeter and not as spicy as Buffalo Wings. If having a party, try making both recipes and offering the Barbecue Wings to your younger guests who may not enjoy the spiced-up version.

- **Total Recipe Cost: $5.96**
- **Hands-On Time: 10 minutes**
- **Cook Time: 15 minutes**

Serves 4

2 pounds frozen chicken wings
½ tablespoon garlic salt
1½ cups water
1 cup barbecue sauce

1 In a large bowl, toss chicken wings in garlic salt so they are evenly coated.

2 Pour water into Instant Pot® and add a trivet.

3 Place wings in a 7" springform pan. Create a foil sling and lower pan into Instant Pot®.

4 Close lid and set pressure release to Sealing.

5 Press Manual or Pressure Cook button and adjust time to 15 minutes.

6 When the timer beeps, allow pressure to release naturally and then unlock lid and remove it. Remove pan from Instant Pot® using foil sling.

7 Remove wings and brush with barbecue sauce. Serve hot.

PER SERVING

CALORIES: 352 | FAT: 16g | PROTEIN: 22g | SODIUM: 801mg
FIBER: 1g | CARBOHYDRATES: 28g | SUGAR: 23g

Buffalo Chicken Dip

This zesty dip tastes like buffalo wings. It tastes great served with celery or crackers.

- **Total Recipe Cost:** $6.06
- **Hands-On Time:** 10 minutes
- **Cook Time:** 15 minutes

Serves 6

1½ cups water

½ pound boneless, skinless chicken breast

8 ounces cream cheese, cut into cubes

1½ cups shredded Cheddar cheese, divided

½ cup ranch dressing

5 tablespoons butter

2 tablespoons Worcestershire sauce

1 tablespoon red wine vinegar

1 Pour water into Instant Pot®. Place trivet inside Instant Pot®.

2 In a 6-cup metal bowl, combine chicken, cream cheese, ½ cup Cheddar cheese, ranch dressing, butter, Worcestershire, and vinegar.

3 Cover bowl with a paper towel and piece of foil, crimped around the edges. Create a foil sling and lower bowl into Instant Pot®.

4 Close lid and set pressure release to Sealing.

5 Press Manual or Pressure Cook button and adjust time to 15 minutes.

6 When the timer beeps, allow pressure to release naturally for 10 minutes and then quick release remaining pressure. Unlock lid and remove it.

7 Carefully lift bowl out of Instant Pot® with foil sling. Remove paper towel and foil from bowl.

8 Remove chicken from bowl and shred with two forks.

9 While dip is still hot, mix in shredded chicken and remaining 1 cup Cheddar cheese. Stir until combined and cheese is melted.

PER SERVING

CALORIES: 468 | FAT: 42g | PROTEIN: 18g | SODIUM: 557mg
FIBER: 0g | CARBOHYDRATES: 5g | SUGAR: 3g

Party Mix

This classic Party Mix tastes great and feeds a crowd. It can be made up to three days in advance. Simply store it in an air-tight container at room temperature.

- **Total Recipe Cost: $10.85**
- **Hands-On Time: 10 minutes**
- **Cook Time: 2½ hours**

Serves 12

4 cups square corn cereal

4 cups square rice cereal

2 cups square wheat cereal

2 cups bagel chips

1 cup small pretzels

1 cup fish-shaped cheese crackers

¼ cup Worcestershire sauce

6 tablespoons butter, melted

3 teaspoons garlic salt

¾ teaspoon onion powder

1 Spray inside of Instant Pot® with cooking spray.

2 Combine corn cereal, rice cereal, wheat cereal, bagel chips, pretzels, and cheese crackers inside Instant Pot®. Stir to combine.

3 In a small bowl, whisk together Worcestershire sauce, butter, garlic salt, and onion powder. Pour over cereal and stir.

4 Place two paper towels overlapping on top of Instant Pot® and top with a glass lid.

5 Press Slow Cook button and program to 2½ hours.

6 Remove lid and stir every 30 minutes.

7 When cooking has completed, pour Party Mix onto a parchment-lined baking pan to cool.

8 Serve at room temperature and store any unused portion in an air-tight container. Party Mix can be stored up to three days.

PER SERVING

CALORIES: 244 | FAT: 9g | PROTEIN: 4g | SODIUM: 368mg
FIBER: 3g | CARBOHYDRATES: 39g | SUGAR: 4g

Muddy Buddies

This simple recipe is made with square corn cereal that is coated in peanut butter, chocolate, and powdered sugar. This sweet snack is light and airy and totally indulgent.

- **Total Recipe Cost: $5.71**
- **Hands-On Time: 5 minutes**
- **Cook Time: 15 minutes**

Serves 6

2 cups water
1 cup semisweet chocolate chips
½ cup smooth peanut butter
¼ cup butter
½ teaspoon vanilla extract
4 cups square rice cereal
1 cup powdered sugar

1 Pour water into Instant Pot® and press Sauté. Bring water to a boil.

2 Place a large metal bowl on the top of Instant Pot® so it is sitting partially inside pot.

3 Place chocolate chips, peanut butter, butter, and vanilla in bowl. Stir constantly until fully melted and smooth, about 15 minutes.

4 Pour in cereal and stir until fully coated.

5 Sprinkle powdered sugar on top and mix until evenly coated.

6 Spread muddy buddies onto parchment-lined baking pan and let cool.

7 Store in an air-tight container at room temperature. Muddy Buddies can be stored up to three days.

PER SERVING

CALORIES: 474 | FAT: 27g | PROTEIN: 8g | SODIUM: 154mg
FIBER: 4g | CARBOHYDRATES: 58g | SUGAR: 38g

Pull-Apart Pizza Bread

This twist on pizza is a fun appetizer made with pizza dough balls coated in seasoning and cheese that you can dip into pizza sauce. It's great for sharing!

- **Total Recipe Cost:** $4.50
- **Hands-On Time:** 15 minutes
- **Cook Time:** 22 minutes

Serves 4

2½ cups all-purpose flour

4 teaspoons baking powder

½ teaspoon salt

1 cup butter, chilled and divided

1 cup whole milk

2 tablespoons Italian seasoning

1 teaspoon chili powder

½ teaspoon garlic powder

1 cup grated Parmesan cheese

1½ cups water

½ cup pizza sauce

WHERE'RE THE TOPPINGS?
This basic pizza bread recipe does not include any toppings. To customize this recipe, gather up to 1 cup of fully cooked toppings and arrange on top of the pizza bread prior to cooking.

1 Spray a 6-cup Bundt pan with cooking spray and set aside.

2 In a medium bowl, whisk together flour, baking powder, and salt.

3 Cut ½ cup butter into small cubes and place into dry ingredients. Use a fork to mix in the butter until dry ingredients are crumbly and about the size of peas.

4 Slowly pour in milk, mixing until a dough forms.

5 Use clean hands to knead the dough about 10 minutes until smooth.

6 Pour dough onto a lightly floured surface and pat into a 10" round. Cut dough up into 1" pieces and set aside.

7 In a gallon-sized zip-top bag, combine Italian seasoning, chili powder, garlic powder, and Parmesan. Close bag and shake to mix.

8 Place cut pieces of dough into bag of spices. Gently knead bag until each piece of dough is coated in spice mixture.

9 Remove dough pieces and arrange evenly in greased Bundt pan.

10 Set Instant Pot® to Sauté. Pour in remaining ½ cup butter. Whisk 1 minute until butter is melted.

11 Turn off Instant Pot®. Pour butter over the top of pizza bread pieces in Bundt pan.

12 Remove cooking pot and clean it. Put it back inside Instant Pot®.

continued on next page

Pull-Apart Pizza Bread (continued)

13 Pour water into Instant Pot® and add trivet.

14 Cover Bundt pan with a paper towel and foil. Crimp edges to discourage water from getting inside pan. Create a foil sling and carefully lower Bundt pan into the Instant Pot®.

15 Close lid and set pressure release to Sealing.

16 Press Manual or Pressure Cook button and adjust time to 21 minutes.

17 When the timer beeps, allow pressure to release naturally for 5 minutes and then quick release remaining pressure. Unlock lid and remove it.

18 Remove Bundt pan using foil sling. Remove foil and paper towel from the top of pan and let cool on a rack 5 minutes.

19 Serve with pizza sauce for dipping.

PER SERVING

CALORIES: 837 | **FAT:** 55g | **PROTEIN:** 19g | **SODIUM:** 1,184mg
FIBER: 4g | **CARBOHYDRATES:** 68g | **SUGAR:** 5g

Spaghetti Sauce

Do you want the taste of homemade spaghetti sauce that has been simmering on the stove all day, but don't want to spend your day camped out in the kitchen? You need this Instant Pot® Spaghetti Sauce recipe in your life! Serve this sauce with your favorite pasta.

- **Total Recipe Cost:** $4.96
- **Hands-On Time:** 10 minutes
- **Cook Time:** 18 minutes

Yields 6 cups

2 tablespoons olive oil

1 medium yellow onion, peeled and chopped

1 pound ground beef

3 cloves garlic, minced

2¼ cups water

1 (15-ounce) can tomato sauce

2 (6-ounce) cans tomato paste

4 teaspoons sugar

2 teaspoons dried basil

1¾ teaspoons salt

1 teaspoon dried oregano

¼ teaspoon crushed red pepper flakes

⅛ teaspoon cayenne pepper

1 bay leaf

1. Set Instant Pot® to Sauté and heat oil.

2. Add in chopped onion and ground beef. Mix and cook until beef is browned and onion is soft, about 7 minutes.

3. Add garlic and cook another 30 seconds.

4. Pour in water and deglaze bottom of pot. Turn Instant Pot® off.

5. Mix in tomato sauce, tomato paste, sugar, basil, salt, oregano, red pepper, cayenne, and bay leaf.

6. Close lid and set pressure release to Sealing.

7. Press Manual or Pressure Cook button and adjust time to 10 minutes.

8. When the timer beeps, allow pressure to release naturally and then unlock lid and remove it. Discard bay leaf and serve.

PER SERVING (½ CUP)

CALORIES: 144 | FAT: 8g | PROTEIN: 9g | SODIUM: 549mg
FIBER: 2g | CARBOHYDRATES: 10g | SUGAR: 7g

Alfredo Sauce

Alfredo Sauce is incredibly easy to make from scratch and tastes so much better than the jarred versions available at the grocery store. Make a batch of this to top pizza or pasta.

- **Total Recipe Cost: $3.29**
- **Hands-On Time: 5 minutes**
- **Cook Time: 10 minutes**

Yields 2 cups

¼ cup unsalted butter

1 cup heavy whipping cream

2 cloves garlic, minced

1½ cups grated Parmesan cheese

½ teaspoon salt

¼ teaspoon black pepper

1. Press Sauté button on Instant Pot®. Add butter and let melt.

2. Once butter is melted, whisk in heavy cream and bring to a simmer, stirring constantly. Cook 5 minutes.

3. Whisk in garlic and Parmesan. Stir 1 minute until cheese is melted.

4. Season with salt and pepper and remove from heat. Use immediately.

PER SERVING (¼ CUP)

CALORIES: 216 | FAT: 21g | PROTEIN: 7g | SODIUM: 409mg
FIBER: 0g | CARBOHYDRATES: 2g | SUGAR: 1g

Béchamel Sauce (Simple White Sauce)

Béchamel Sauce is considered one of the mother sauces of French cuisine. It is a basic white sauce that can be used in casseroles, made into a cheese sauce, or used in place of cream of mushroom soup in recipes. This recipe can be made and frozen for future use.

- **Total Recipe Cost:** $0.83
- **Hands-On Time:** 5 minutes
- **Cook Time:** 10 minutes

Yields 2 cups

4 tablespoons butter
4 tablespoons all-purpose flour
½ teaspoon salt
¼ teaspoon black pepper
2 cups whole milk

1 Set Instant Pot® to Sauté and melt butter.

2 Whisk in flour and cook 3 minutes until golden brown.

3 Mix in salt and pepper.

4 Slowly pour in milk, whisking constantly so mixture does not become lumpy.

5 Cook an additional 5 minutes until thickened, stirring constantly.

6 Remove from heat and use as needed.

PER SERVING (¼ CUP)

CALORIES: 103 | FAT: 8g | PROTEIN: 2g | SODIUM: 172mg
FIBER: 0g | CARBOHYDRATES: 6g | SUGAR: 3g

Peach Freezer Jam

Savor the summer season all year long with this delicious Peach Freezer Jam recipe. Freezer jam stays fresh up to one month in the refrigerator and three months in the freezer.

- **Total Recipe Cost:** $7.73
- **Hands-On Time:** 15 minutes
- **Cook Time:** 1 minute

Yields 4 pints

6 cups chopped peaches, peeled and pitted

4 cups sugar

1 (1.75-ounce) packet pectin

1 tablespoon lemon juice

THE SPOON TRICK

Every once in a while, homemade jam does not gel up as it should. Here is a foolproof way to ensure your peaches turn into jam. While your jam is cooking, place a metal spoon in the freezer. After removing the lid from your Instant Pot®, take a spoonful of jam with the frozen spoon and turn the spoon sideways. The jam should immediately gel up and not slide instantly off the spoon. If the jam does not gel, turn the Instant Pot® on to Sauté and bring the jam to a boil. Let it boil 1 minute before removing from heat.

1 In a large bowl, mash chopped peaches with a potato masher. Places mashed peaches inside Instant Pot®.

2 Pour sugar over peaches and let sit 2–3 minutes until the juices have been released.

3 Mix in pectin and lemon juice.

4 Close the lid and set pressure release to Sealing.

5 Press Manual or Pressure Cook button and adjust time to 1 minute.

6 When the timer beeps, allow pressure to release naturally. Unlock lid and remove it.

7 Spoon into pint-sized canning jars, leaving 1" of space between jam and lid.

8 Let cool and then refrigerate or freeze.

PER SERVING (1 TABLESPOON)

CALORIES: 28 | FAT: 0g | PROTEIN: 0g | SODIUM: 1mg
FIBER: 0g | CARBOHYDRATES: 7g | SUGAR: 7g

6

Side Dishes

Sides dishes can really make a meal shine. This chapter will share many frugal side dishes that taste great, including Artichokes with Dipping Sauce, Corn Bread, and Garlic Mashed Potatoes. You will love making sides with your Instant Pot® because you can set it and forget it while still ending up with a delicious and well-balanced meal.

Corn on the Cob

Cooking Corn on the Cob in the Instant Pot® is so much faster than making it on the stove. More corn can be added while keeping the cook time the same.

- **Total Recipe Cost: $2.01**
- **Hands-On Time: 5 minutes**
- **Cook Time: 5 minutes**

Serves 4

1 cup water
¼ teaspoon salt
4 ears corn

TYPES OF CORN

Deciding between white and yellow corn can be a bit confusing. Both are good but the white variety is sweeter. White corn is the way to go if you have the choice.

1 Pour water and salt into Instant Pot® and add trivet. Place corn on top of the trivet.

2 Close lid and set pressure release to Sealing.

3 Press Manual or Pressure Cook button and adjust time to 5 minutes.

4 When the timer beeps, quick release pressure and then unlock lid and remove it.

5 Serve corn.

PER SERVING

CALORIES: 77 | FAT: 1g | PROTEIN: 3g | SODIUM: 159mg
FIBER: 2g | CARBOHYDRATES: 17g | SUGAR: 3g

Sweet Potatoes

Save time with this recipe for Sweet Potatoes in the Instant Pot®. They come out sweet and tender every time, in just 15 minutes! We like to serve ours with a little bit of brown sugar sprinkled on top.

- **Total Recipe Cost:** $4.09
- **Hands-On Time:** 5 minutes
- **Cook Time:** 15 minutes

Serves 4

1 cup water
4 medium sweet potatoes

1 Pour water into Instant Pot® and add trivet.

2 Pierce sweet potatoes with a fork on both sides, top and bottom. Place sweet potatoes on top of the trivet.

3 Close lid and set pressure release to Sealing.

4 Press Manual or Pressure Cook button and adjust time to 15 minutes.

5 When the timer beeps, quick release pressure and then unlock lid and remove it.

6 Serve.

PER SERVING

CALORIES: 112 | FAT: 0g | PROTEIN: 2g | SODIUM: 72mg
FIBER: 4g | CARBOHYDRATES: 26g | SUGAR: 5g

"Baked" Potatoes

This is another easy recipe that saves time. This "Baked" Potatoes recipe can be doubled with the same cook time. Just stack the potatoes on top of each other. If using large potatoes, cook for an additional 10 minutes.

- **Total Recipe Cost: $1.21**
- **Hands-On Time: 5 minutes**
- **Cook Time: 20 minutes**

Serves 4

1 cup water
½ teaspoon salt
4 medium russet potatoes

1 Pour water and salt into Instant Pot® and add trivet.

2 Pierce potatoes with a fork on both sides, top and bottom. Place potatoes on top of the trivet.

3 Close lid and set pressure release to Sealing.

4 Press Manual or Pressure Cook button and adjust time to 20 minutes.

5 When the timer beeps, quick release pressure and then unlock lid and remove it.

6 Serve potatoes.

PER SERVING

CALORIES: 168 | FAT: 0g | PROTEIN: 5g | SODIUM: 301mg
FIBER: 3g | CARBOHYDRATES: 38g | SUGAR: 1g

Red Potato Salad

This classic side dish cooks up quickly in the Instant Pot®. It is made with a handful of simple ingredients that make it the perfect addition to a barbecue or picnic.

- **Total Recipe Cost:** $2.68
- **Hands-On Time:** 20 minutes
- **Cook Time:** 4 minutes

Serves 6

1 cup water

2½ pounds medium red potatoes, peeled and cut into 1" cubes

½ cup mayonnaise

2 tablespoons yellow mustard

1 tablespoon apple cider vinegar

½ teaspoon salt

½ teaspoon black pepper

½ teaspoon paprika

4 medium green onions, sliced

1 Pour water into Instant Pot®. Place trivet and steamer basket inside Instant Pot®.

2 Arrange cubed potatoes inside steamer basket.

3 Close lid and set pressure release to Sealing.

4 Press Manual or Pressure Cook button and adjust time to 4 minutes.

5 When the timer beeps, quick release the pressure and then unlock lid and remove it.

6 Remove potatoes from Instant Pot® and place into a bowl of ice water. Let sit 10 minutes.

7 In a small bowl, whisk together mayonnaise, mustard, vinegar, salt, pepper, and paprika.

8 Remove potatoes from ice bath and place in a large, dry bowl.

9 Pour sauce over potatoes and stir until fully coated. Toss potato salad with sliced green onions.

10 Chill until ready to serve.

PER SERVING

CALORIES: 288 | **FAT:** 14g | **PROTEIN:** 4g | **SODIUM:** 378mg
FIBER: 4g | **CARBOHYDRATES:** 37g | **SUGAR:** 2g

Zucchini Fritters

Enjoy the flavors of the season with this tasty zucchini recipe. Mixed with cheese and flour and fried, these Zucchini Fritters are a side dish with loads of flavor.

- **Total Recipe Cost: $2.28**
- **Hands-On Time: 15 minutes**
- **Cook Time: 24 minutes**

Serves 4

4 cups shredded zucchini
1 teaspoon salt
1 large egg, beaten
⅓ cup all-purpose flour
⅓ cup shredded Parmesan cheese
2 cloves garlic, minced
½ teaspoon black pepper
6 tablespoons olive oil

1 Place zucchini in a colander and sprinkle with salt. Let sit 10 minutes.

2 Remove zucchini from colander and wrap in a clean dish towel. Squeeze and wring water out of zucchini.

3 Place zucchini in a large bowl with egg, flour, Parmesan, garlic, and pepper. Mix well to combine.

4 Push Sauté button on Instant Pot®. Pour 2 tablespoons oil into Instant Pot®.

5 Take heaping tablespoons of zucchini and place in Instant Pot®. Flatten out with back of spoon into 2½" rounds. Work in batches, making three fritters at a time.

6 Let cook 4 minutes and then flip. Cook an additional 4 minutes on the second side.

7 Remove Zucchini Fritters using a slotted spatula. Continue cooking until all zucchini is used up, adding additional oil with each batch.

8 Serve hot.

PER SERVING

CALORIES: 300 | FAT: 25g | PROTEIN: 8g | SODIUM: 489mg
FIBER: 1g | CARBOHYDRATES: 13g | SUGAR: 3g

Garlic Mashed Potatoes

Preminced garlic in a jar works wonderfully in this recipe. Use heaping teaspoons in place of each clove.

- **Total Recipe Cost: $2.17**
- **Hands-On Time:** 10 minutes
- **Cook Time:** 8 minutes

Serves 4

2½ pounds russet potatoes, peeled
1 cup chicken broth
½ teaspoon salt
¾ cup whole milk, warm
2 tablespoons butter
5 cloves garlic, minced

1 Pour potatoes, broth, and salt inside Instant Pot®.

2 Close lid and set pressure release to Sealing.

3 Press Manual or Pressure Cook button and adjust time to 8 minutes.

4 When the timer beeps, quick release pressure and then unlock lid and remove it.

5 Drain broth and discard.

6 Use a potato masher to mash potatoes in the pot. Pour in warm milk and mix.

7 Mix in butter until melted. Fold in garlic.

8 Serve warm.

PER SERVING

CALORIES: 320 | **FAT:** 8g | **PROTEIN:** 7g | **SODIUM:** 348mg
FIBER: 5g | **CARBOHYDRATES:** 57g | **SUGAR:** 5g

Sweet Potato Casserole

Say hello to your new favorite Thanksgiving side dish! This Instant Pot® Sweet Potato Casserole is insanely easy to make and tastes so good thanks to the creamy sweet potatoes, sweet orange juice, and toasted marshmallows.

- **Total Recipe Cost: $5.07**
- **Hands-On Time: 10 minutes**
- **Cook Time: 23 minutes**

Serves 6

1 cup water
3 (15-ounce) cans sweet potatoes, drained
½ cup packed brown sugar
¼ cup butter, melted
3 tablespoons orange juice
⅛ teaspoon ground cinnamon
1 (10-ounce) bag mini marshmallows

USING FRESH SWEET POTATOES

If you prefer, you can also use fresh sweet potatoes in this recipe. The sweet potatoes should be cooked as described in the Sweet Potatoes recipe in this chapter, peeled, and cubed into 2" chunks. Then they may be used in place of canned sweet potatoes.

1 Pour water into Instant Pot® and add trivet. Grease a 7" cake pan and set aside.

2 In a large bowl, place sweet potatoes, brown sugar, butter, orange juice, and cinnamon. Mix until fully combined.

3 Pour sweet potato mixture into cake pan. Top with half of the bag of mini marshmallows.

4 Cover cake pan with a dry paper towel and a piece of foil. Secure foil over the pan so the paper towel does not slip.

5 Create a foil sling and carefully lower the covered cake pan into the Instant Pot® and fold the ends of the foil sling over the cake pan.

6 Close lid and set pressure release to Sealing.

7 Press Manual or Pressure Cook button and adjust time to 20 minutes.

8 When the timer beeps, quick release pressure and then unlock lid and remove it.

9 Carefully remove cake pan using foil sling. Remove foil and paper towel.

10 Arrange the remaining half of mini marshmallows on top of casserole.

11 Broil casserole in oven 2–3 minutes until marshmallows begin to brown. Watch carefully to ensure marshmallows do not burn. Serve.

PER SERVING

CALORIES: 481 | FAT: 8g | PROTEIN: 3g | SODIUM: 106mg
FIBER: 5g | CARBOHYDRATES: 102g | SUGAR: 78g

Artichokes with Dipping Sauce

The Instant Pot® is the easiest and fastest way to steam artichokes. They are made even better with the tasty dipping sauce.

- **Total Recipe Cost: $6.39**
- **Hands-On Time: 10 minutes**
- **Cook Time: 15 minutes**

Serves 4

2 large artichokes
1 medium lemon
1 cup water
3 cloves garlic, crushed
¾ teaspoon salt, divided
3 tablespoons mayonnaise
¼ teaspoon chili powder
⅛ teaspoon black pepper

VARYING ARTICHOKE SIZES
Large artichokes may not always be available at your local grocery store. If that is the case, adjust the cook time as follows: 5 minutes for small artichokes and 10 minutes for medium artichokes.

1 Rinse artichokes and slice off top ½" of each artichoke.

2 Cut lemon in half. Set one half aside. Cut the other half into wedges.

3 Fill Instant Pot® with water, garlic, lemon wedges, and ½ teaspoon salt.

4 Place trivet into Instant Pot® and arrange artichokes on top. Trim artichoke stems, if needed for lid to close.

5 Close lid and set pressure release to Sealing.

6 Press Manual or Pressure Cook button and adjust time to 15 minutes.

7 When the timer beeps, quick release pressure and then unlock lid and remove it. Remove artichokes.

8 In a small bowl, whisk together mayonnaise, juice from remaining ½ lemon, remaining ¼ teaspoon salt, chili powder, and pepper.

9 Cut artichokes in half and serve with sauce.

PER SERVING

CALORIES: 115 | FAT: 8g | PROTEIN: 3g | SODIUM: 438mg
FIBER: 5g | CARBOHYDRATES: 10g | SUGAR: 1g

Green Beans with Shallots

Here is a quick and easy fresh green bean recipe paired perfectly with mild and sweet caramelized shallots. These green beans taste great when paired with both salmon and beef.

- **Total Recipe Cost: $3.74**
- **Hands-On Time: 5 minutes**
- **Cook Time: 6 minutes**

Serves 4

1 cup water
¾ teaspoon salt, divided
1 pound green beans, trimmed
2 tablespoons olive oil
1 medium shallot, peeled and minced
½ teaspoon black pepper

1 Pour water and ½ teaspoon salt into Instant Pot® and add steamer basket. Place green beans on top of steamer basket.

2 Close lid and set pressure release to Sealing.

3 Press Steam button and adjust time to 0 minutes.

4 When the timer beeps, quick release pressure and then unlock lid and remove it. Remove green beans. Drain water.

5 Press Sauté button and add oil to the pot.

6 Add shallot and green beans. Let cook, stirring occasionally, 6 minutes.

7 Season with remaining ¼ teaspoon salt and pepper. Remove from heat and serve.

PER SERVING

CALORIES: 102 | FAT: 7g | PROTEIN: 2g | SODIUM: 299mg
FIBER: 3g | CARBOHYDRATES: 10g | SUGAR: 4g

Curried Cauliflower

This recipe for Curried Cauliflower is an easy dish to make in the Instant Pot®. Sautéing the cauliflower in the Instant Pot® deepens and sweetens its flavor.

- **Total Recipe Cost: $3.50**
- **Hands-On Time: 5 minutes**
- **Cook Time: 13 minutes**

Serves 4

2 tablespoons olive oil
1 medium head cauliflower, cut into florets
½ teaspoon curry powder
⅛ teaspoon salt
⅛ teaspoon black pepper

1 Press Sauté button. Pour in oil and let heat 1 minute.

2 Add cauliflower, curry powder, salt, and pepper and stir to combine. Cover and let cook 12 minutes, stirring occasionally.

3 Remove from heat and serve hot.

PER SERVING

CALORIES: 97 | FAT: 7g | PROTEIN: 3g | SODIUM: 117mg
FIBER: 3g | CARBOHYDRATES: 7g | SUGAR: 3g

Broccoli and Garlic

This is a simple and flavorful side dish made with broccoli florets and whole garlic cloves pan roasted in olive oil. It tastes great served with Hawaiian Chicken (see recipe in Chapter 7).

- **Total Recipe Cost: $2.71**
- **Hands-On Time: 5 minutes**
- **Cook Time: 9 minutes**

Serves 4

3 tablespoons olive oil
2 medium heads broccoli, cut into florets
½ teaspoon salt
½ teaspoon black pepper
4 cloves garlic, crushed

1 Press Sauté button. Pour in oil and let heat 1 minute.

2 Mix in broccoli, salt, and pepper. Cover and let cook 4 minutes, stirring occasionally.

3 Mix in garlic and cover with lid. Let cook an additional 4 minutes, stirring occasionally.

4 Remove from heat and serve hot.

PER SERVING

CALORIES: 198 | FAT: 11g | PROTEIN: 9g | SODIUM: 392mg
FIBER: 8g | CARBOHYDRATES: 21g | SUGAR: 5g

Strawberry Applesauce

Skip the store and make a batch of this delicious Strawberry Applesauce at home instead! With just five ingredients and a 5-minute pressure-cooking time, this Instant Pot® applesauce recipe is a winner!

- **Total Recipe Cost: $8.06**
- **Hands-On Time:** 10 minutes
- **Cook Time:** 5 minutes

Serves 6

6 cups roughly chopped Gala apples
4 cups frozen strawberries
½ cup granulated sugar
½ cup water
¼ teaspoon salt

MAKING TRADITIONAL APPLE SAUCE

If you prefer the classic apple sauce flavor, you can omit the strawberries and replace with 4 additional cups of apples. A combination of green and red apples would work wonderfully for a sweet-tart applesauce.

1 Add apples and strawberries to Instant Pot®.

2 Pour in sugar, water, and salt. Mix well to combine.

3 Close lid and set pressure release to Sealing.

4 Press Manual or Pressure Cook button and adjust time to 5 minutes.

5 When the timer beeps, allow the pressure to release naturally and then unlock lid and remove it.

6 Using an immersion blender, blend mixture until smooth.

7 Chill in the refrigerator 2 hours. Serve cold.

PER SERVING

CALORIES: 165 | FAT: 0g | PROTEIN: 1g | SODIUM: 100mg
FIBER: 5g | CARBOHYDRATES: 43g | SUGAR: 34g

Honey Carrots

These sweetened carrots come out quite tender in the Instant Pot®. They are very kid-friendly and taste great paired with chicken or pork.

- **Total Recipe Cost: $2.08**
- **Hands-On Time: 10 minutes**
- **Cook Time: 16 minutes**

Serves 4

⅓ cup olive oil

1 pound carrots, cut into ½"
   slices

1 teaspoon cumin

½ teaspoon salt

¼ teaspoon black pepper

¼ cup honey

1 Press Sauté button. Pour in oil and let heat 1 minute.

2 Add carrots, cumin, salt, and pepper. Cover and let cook 10 minutes, stirring occasionally.

3 Mix in honey and cover with a lid. Let cook an additional 5 minutes, stirring occasionally.

4 Remove from heat and serve hot.

PER SERVING

CALORIES: 266 | FAT: 18g | PROTEIN: 1g | SODIUM: 362mg
FIBER: 3g | CARBOHYDRATES: 37g | SUGAR: 22g

Mashed Cauliflower

Mashed Cauliflower tastes very similar to mashed potatoes. It's a fun way to get an extra serving of vegetables. With a 2-minute cook time, it can be made quickly, thanks to the Instant Pot®.

- **Total Recipe Cost: $3.27**
- **Hands-On Time: 10 minutes**
- **Cook Time: 2 minutes**

Serves 4

1 cup water
1 medium head cauliflower, cut into florets
1 cup whole milk, warm
1 tablespoon unsalted butter
¼ teaspoon salt

1 Pour water into Instant Pot®. Place trivet and steamer basket inside Instant Pot®.

2 Arrange cauliflower on top of steamer basket.

3 Close lid and set pressure release to Sealing.

4 Press Manual or Pressure Cook button and adjust time to 2 minutes.

5 When the timer beeps, quick release pressure and then unlock lid and remove it.

6 Drain water and remove trivet and steamer basket.

7 Place cauliflower into bottom of Instant Pot®. Mash cauliflower with a potato masher until smooth.

8 Mix in warm milk and stir until cauliflower absorbs milk.

9 Fold in butter and salt. Mix until butter is melted. Serve warm.

PER SERVING

CALORIES: 99 | FAT: 5g | PROTEIN: 5g | SODIUM: 216mg
FIBER: 3g | CARBOHYDRATES: 10g | SUGAR: 6g

Sweet Corn Tamalito

This sweet corn dish is a favorite at several Mexican chain restaurants. It's traditionally steamed in a double boiler, making it a perfect recipe for the Instant Pot®.

- **Total Recipe Cost:** $2.33
- **Hands-On Time:** 15 minutes
- **Cook Time:** 50 minutes

Serves 6

5 tablespoons butter, melted
¼ cup masa harina
½ cup granulated sugar
2½ cups water, divided
2 cups frozen corn kernels, thawed, divided
½ cup cornmeal
4 teaspoons whole milk
1 teaspoon baking powder
½ teaspoon salt

WHAT IS MASA HARINA?

Masa harina is a corn flour that is cooked in an alkaline solution before being dried. It's used in many Latin dishes, including tamales and corn tortillas. When looking for this product in store, it may be called simply masa, masaca, or corn masa.

1 In a large bowl, whisk together butter, masa harina, and sugar until fluffy.

2 In a blender, combine ½ cup water, 1 cup corn, and cornmeal. Blend until smooth.

3 Mix the blended corn into the masa mixture.

4 Whisk in remaining 1 cup corn, milk, baking powder, and salt. Stir until fully combined.

5 Pour batter into a 7-cup metal bowl. Place a paper towel on top of the bowl and cover tightly with foil.

6 Pour remaining 2 cups water into Instant Pot®. Place trivet inside. Create a foil sling and carefully lower bowl into Instant Pot®.

7 Close lid and set to Sealing.

8 Press Steam button and adjust time to 50 minutes.

9 When the timer beeps, quick release pressure and then unlock lid and remove it.

10 Remove bowl using foil sling. Take off paper towel and foil.

11 Stir before serving.

PER SERVING

CALORIES: 239 | **FAT:** 10g | **PROTEIN:** 2g | **SODIUM:** 290mg
FIBER: 3g | **CARBOHYDRATES:** 36g | **SUGAR:** 18g

Corn Bread

This Corn Bread comes out perfectly moist every time in the Instant Pot®. Feel free to mix in your favorite add-ins like jalapeños or sharp Cheddar.

- **Total Recipe Cost: $2.37**
- **Hands-On Time:** 10 minutes
- **Cook Time:** 25 minutes

Serves 6

1 cup water
1½ cups all-purpose flour
¾ cup cornmeal
2 cups granulated sugar
2 teaspoons baking powder
½ teaspoon salt
1 large egg, beaten
1 cup whole milk
½ cup vegetable oil
½ cup frozen corn kernels, thawed

1 Pour water into Instant Pot® and add trivet. Grease a 6-cup Bundt pan and set aside.

2 In a large bowl, whisk together flour, corn-meal, sugar, baking powder, and salt.

3 Make a well in center of dry ingredients and pour in egg, milk, and oil. Fold dry ingredients into wet ingredients until just combined.

4 Add in corn and mix until evenly distributed.

5 Pour corn bread batter into Bundt pan. Cover pan with a paper towel and then tightly with foil.

6 Create a foil sling and carefully lower Bundt pan into Instant Pot®.

7 Close lid and set pressure release to Sealing.

8 Press Manual or Pressure Cook button and adjust time to 25 minutes.

9 When the timer beeps, allow pressure to release naturally for 10 minutes and then quick release remaining pressure. Unlock lid and remove it. Remove pan from Instant Pot® using foil sling.

10 Let cool on a wire rack before serving.

PER SERVING

CALORIES: 635 | **FAT:** 21g | **PROTEIN:** 7g | **SODIUM:** 351mg
FIBER: 4g | **CARBOHYDRATES:** 107g | **SUGAR:** 69g

Zucchini Corn Casserole

Part corn bread, part casserole, this Zucchini Corn Casserole is a great way to use up excess zucchini. It is a great side dish with chili or grilled meat.

- **Total Recipe Cost: $4.71**
- **Hands-On Time:** 15 minutes
- **Cook Time:** 65 minutes

Serves 6

1½ cups water
1½ cups all-purpose flour
¾ cup cornmeal
2 teaspoons baking powder
1 teaspoon salt
¼ teaspoon black pepper
2 large eggs, beaten
1 cup whole milk
¼ cup vegetable oil
4 cups shredded zucchini
1½ cups Monterey jack cheese

1. Pour water into Instant Pot® and add trivet. Grease a 7" cake pan and set aside.

2. In a large bowl, whisk together flour, cornmeal, baking powder, salt, and pepper.

3. Create a well inside the dry ingredients and pour in egg, milk, and oil. Mix well.

4. Mix in zucchini until fully combined. Then fold in cheese.

5. Pour casserole batter into cake pan. Top with a paper towel and cover top of pan tightly with foil. Create a foil sling and carefully lower cake pan into Instant Pot®.

6. Close lid and set pressure release to Sealing.

7. Press Manual or Pressure Cook button and adjust time to 65 minutes.

8. When the timer beeps, quick release pressure and then unlock lid and remove it. Remove pan from Instant Pot® using foil sling.

9. Serve hot.

PER SERVING

CALORIES: 409 | FAT: 21g | PROTEIN: 15g | SODIUM: 437mg
FIBER: 4g | CARBOHYDRATES: 39g | SUGAR: 3g

Vegetable Tian

This dish is a combination of squash, zucchini, tomato, and potato, sliced thinly and cooked in minced onion and garlic. It pairs nicely with Spinach and Feta–Stuffed Tilapia (see recipe in Chapter 9).

- **Total Recipe Cost:** $3.53
- **Hands-On Time:** 10 minutes
- **Cook Time:** 30 minutes

Serves 4

1 tablespoon olive oil

½ medium yellow onion, peeled and diced

2 cloves garlic, minced

1 cup water

1 medium yellow squash, cut into ½"-thick slices

1 medium zucchini, cut into ½"-thick slices

2 Roma tomatoes, cut into ½"-thick slices

1 large russet potato, cut into ½"-thick slices

¼ teaspoon salt

⅛ teaspoon black pepper

½ cup shredded mozzarella cheese

¼ cup grated Parmesan cheese

1 Press Sauté button on Instant Pot®.

2 Add oil and onion. Let cook 4 minutes or until onion is soft.

3 Add garlic and cook an additional 30 seconds until fragrant.

4 Remove garlic and onion and spread in the bottom of a 7" cake pan.

5 Clean inner pot and place back inside Instant Pot®. Add water and trivet to pot.

6 Arrange sliced vegetables in a pattern of squash, zucchini, tomato, and potato around the edge of the cake pan. Continue in the center of the pan until the vegetables are all used.

7 Top with a paper towel and cover top of pan tightly with foil. Create a foil sling and carefully lower cake pan into Instant Pot®.

8 Close lid and set pressure release to Sealing.

9 Press Manual or Pressure Cook button and adjust time to 30 minutes.

10 When the timer beeps, allow pressure to release naturally for 10 minutes. Quick release remaining pressure and then unlock lid and remove it.

11 Remove pan from Instant Pot® using foil sling. Sprinkle salt, pepper, mozzarella, and Parmesan on top. Serve warm.

PER SERVING

CALORIES: 196 | FAT: 8g | PROTEIN: 9g | SODIUM: 260mg
FIBER: 3g | CARBOHYDRATES: 23g | SUGAR: 4g

Chicken Main Dishes

Chicken is a staple in many frugal kitchens because it is so versatile and filling. This chapter will show you how to quickly whip together a chicken dish that is easy to make and tastes great. Many of these recipes have very little hands-on time too. From Salsa Chicken Tacos to Bacon Ranch Chicken Sandwiches, you are sure to find a recipe that fits your needs.

Whole Chicken

Instant Pot® Whole Chicken is an easy way to make roasted chicken at home in under an hour without the use of your oven.

- **Total Recipe Cost: $7.88**
- **Hands-On Time: 10 minutes**
- **Cook Time: 40 minutes**

Serves 6

1 (6-pound) whole chicken
1 teaspoon salt
½ teaspoon black pepper
½ teaspoon paprika
½ teaspoon garlic powder
1 tablespoon olive oil
1 cup water

DIFFERENT-SIZED CHICKENS

To figure out cook time for a different-sized chicken, calculate 6 minutes per pound of bird and add 2 minutes.

1 Remove giblets from chicken and discard giblets.

2 In a small bowl, mix together salt, pepper, paprika, and garlic powder. Rub spice mixture on chicken.

3 Press Sauté button and pour oil into Instant Pot®.

4 Add chicken and brown both sides of chicken in Instant Pot®, about 1 minute per side. Turn off Instant Pot® and remove chicken.

5 Pour water into Instant Pot® and add trivet. Place chicken on top of trivet.

6 Close lid and set pressure release to Sealing.

7 Press Manual or Pressure Cook button and adjust time to 38 minutes.

8 When the timer beeps, allow pressure to release naturally and then unlock lid and remove it.

9 Serve chicken hot or cold.

PER SERVING

CALORIES: 495 | **FAT:** 28g | **PROTEIN:** 56g | **SODIUM:** 441mg
FIBER: 0g | **CARBOHYDRATES:** 0g | **SUGAR:** 0g

Hawaiian Chicken

This easy three-ingredient recipe tastes great on its own or served over rice. It's also incredibly easy to make—just dump it all in and press start.

- **Total Recipe Cost: $4.81**
- **Hands-On Time:** 5 minutes
- **Cook Time:** 15 minutes

Serves 4

1 pound boneless, skinless chicken breasts
1 (20-ounce) can crushed pineapple
1 (18-ounce) bottle barbecue sauce

1 Add chicken, pineapple (with juice), and barbecue sauce to the Instant Pot®. Stir to combine.

2 Close lid and set pressure release to Sealing.

3 Press Manual or Pressure Cook button and adjust time to 15 minutes.

4 When the timer beeps, allow pressure to release naturally and then unlock lid and remove it.

5 Serve.

PER SERVING

CALORIES: 441 | FAT: 4g | PROTEIN: 27g | SODIUM: 1,363mg
FIBER: 2g | CARBOHYDRATES: 74g | SUGAR: 63g

Easy Shredded Chicken

Learn how to make simple shredded chicken so you can have it on hand whenever you need it! It's great on salads and in other recipes like Sour Cream Enchiladas (see recipe in this chapter).

- **Total Recipe Cost:** $2.57
- **Hands-On Time:** 10 minutes
- **Cook Time:** 15 minutes

Serves 4

1 pound boneless, skinless chicken breasts
1½ cups chicken broth
1 teaspoon salt
¼ teaspoon black pepper

1 Place chicken, broth, salt, and pepper into Instant Pot®.

2 Close lid and set pressure release to Sealing.

3 Press Manual or Pressure Cook button and adjust time to 15 minutes.

4 When the timer beeps, allow pressure to release naturally and then unlock lid and remove it.

5 Remove chicken from Instant Pot® and shred with two forks. Use in any recipe calling for cooked chicken.

PER SERVING

CALORIES: 147 | FAT: 3g | PROTEIN: 27g | SODIUM: 666mg
FIBER: 0g | CARBOHYDRATES: 1g | SUGAR: 0g

Salsa Chicken Tacos

Switch up taco night with these crowd-pleasing Salsa Chicken Tacos. The combination of chunky salsa and taco seasoning packs loads of flavor into the tender chicken. These chicken tacos can be made with fresh or frozen chicken breasts. Simply add 10 minutes of pressure cook time if using frozen chicken breasts.

- **Total Recipe Cost:** $7.00
- **Hands-On Time:** 5 minutes
- **Cook Time:** 10 minutes

Serves 4

2 cups chunky salsa

1 cup chicken broth

1 (1-ounce) packet taco seasoning

1 pound boneless, skinless chicken breasts

8 crunchy taco shells

2 cups shredded romaine lettuce

1 cup grated Mexican-blend cheese

1 In a medium bowl, combine chunky salsa, broth, and taco seasoning. Whisk to combine. Pour salsa mixture into Instant Pot®.

2 Add chicken breast to Instant Pot® and stir.

3 Close lid and set pressure release to Sealing.

4 Press Manual or Pressure Cook button and adjust time to 10 minutes.

5 When the timer beeps, allow pressure to release naturally for 10 minutes and then quick release remaining pressure. Unlock lid and remove it.

6 Use two forks to shred chicken.

7 Serve chicken in taco shells topped with shredded lettuce and cheese.

PER SERVING

CALORIES: 447 | FAT: 19g | PROTEIN: 38g | SODIUM: 2,017mg
FIBER: 6g | CARBOHYDRATES: 32g | SUGAR: 9g

Buffalo Chicken

A delicious spin on traditional buffalo wings made quickly in the Instant Pot®. Serve this with mashed cauliflower and a green salad.

- **Total Recipe Cost: $2.94**
- **Hands-On Time:** 10 minutes
- **Cook Time:** 15 minutes

Serves 4

¾ cup mild hot sauce

3 tablespoons butter, melted

1 tablespoon Worcestershire sauce

½ tablespoon red wine vinegar

½ teaspoon cornstarch

1 pound boneless, skinless chicken breasts

1 In the Instant Pot®, whisk together hot sauce, butter, Worcestershire, vinegar, and cornstarch.

2 Place chicken in Instant Pot® and turn to coat in sauce.

3 Close lid and set pressure release to Sealing.

4 Press Manual or Pressure Cook button and adjust time to 15 minutes.

5 When the timer beeps, allow pressure to release naturally and then unlock lid and remove it.

6 Serve.

PER SERVING

CALORIES: 295 | FAT: 12g | PROTEIN: 26g | SODIUM: 556mg
FIBER: 0g | CARBOHYDRATES: 19g | SUGAR: 15g

Sweet and Sour Chicken

Make takeout at home with this yummy (and quick) recipe for Sweet and Sour Chicken.

- **Total Recipe Cost:** $7.27
- **Hands-On Time:** 10 minutes
- **Cook Time:** 7 minutes

Serves 6

1 cup apple cider vinegar

1 cup granulated sugar

½ cup ketchup

2 tablespoons soy sauce

1½ teaspoons garlic powder

1 teaspoon salt

1 cup cornstarch

2 pounds boneless, skinless chicken breasts, cut into 1" chunks

½ teaspoon salt

¼ teaspoon black pepper

¼ cup vegetable oil

3 large eggs, beaten

1 In a small bowl, whisk together vinegar, sugar, ketchup, soy sauce, garlic powder, and salt. Set aside.

2 Pour cornstarch into a gallon-sized zip-top bag.

3 Season chicken with salt and pepper and place inside the bag of cornstarch. Close bag and shake until chicken is coated evenly.

4 Press Sauté button on Instant Pot®. Pour in oil and let heat 1 minute.

5 Working in batches, remove chicken pieces from bag and dip into beaten eggs.

6 Shake to remove any excess egg, then layer chicken evenly in hot oil on the bottom of pot. Let cook, unmoved, for 30 seconds.

7 Flip and cook another 30 seconds.

8 Remove from pot and continue with remaining chicken.

9 Once chicken is cooked and removed from Instant Pot®, pour sauce into pot and deglaze the pot.

10 Add chicken and turn to coat with sauce.

11 Close lid and set pressure release to Sealing.

12 Press Manual or Pressure Cook button and adjust time to 3 minutes.

13 When the timer beeps, allow pressure to release naturally and then unlock lid and remove it. Serve warm.

PER SERVING

CALORIES: 515 | **FAT:** 15g | **PROTEIN:** 37g | **SODIUM:** 1,130mg
FIBER: 0g | **CARBOHYDRATES:** 56g | **SUGAR:** 39g

Bacon Ranch Chicken Sandwiches

This creamy, cheesy chicken dish is so tasty, it's hard not to come back for seconds. If you do find yourself with leftovers, try it over salad or on crackers.

- **Total Recipe Cost:** $10.41
- **Hands-On Time:** 5 minutes
- **Cook Time:** 20 minutes

Serves 6

½ pound bacon, chopped
1 cup chicken broth
1 (1-ounce) ranch seasoning packet
1 pound boneless, skinless chicken breasts
1 (8-ounce) package cream cheese
1 tablespoon cornstarch
½ cup shredded sharp Cheddar cheese
¼ cup sliced green onions
6 hamburger buns

1 Press Sauté button.

2 Place chopped bacon into Instant Pot® and cook 5 minutes until browned. Remove bacon and place in between two paper towels. Reserve some for garnishing later.

3 Pour broth into Instant Pot® to deglaze bottom of pot.

4 Whisk ranch seasoning packet into broth. Place chicken in pot and top with cream cheese.

5 Close lid and set pressure release to Sealing.

6 Press Manual or Pressure Cook button and adjust time to 15 minutes.

7 When the timer beeps, allow pressure to release naturally for 10 minutes and then quick release remaining pressure. Unlock lid and remove it.

8 Remove chicken and shred with two forks.

9 While chicken is removed, whisk cornstarch into sauce.

10 Return chicken and bacon to the pot and mix until evenly coated with the sauce.

11 Top with Cheddar, green onions, and reserved bacon. Serve on hamburger buns.

PER SERVING

CALORIES: 566 | **FAT:** 35g | **PROTEIN:** 31g | **SODIUM:** 1,052mg
FIBER: 1g | **CARBOHYDRATES:** 29g | **SUGAR:** 5g

Teriyaki Chicken

This classic chicken dish is easy to make and tastes great served on its own with a simple vegetable side or on top of rice.

- **Total Recipe Cost: $3.13**
- **Hands-On Time: 5 minutes**
- **Cook Time: 15 minutes**

Serves 4

½ cup soy sauce
½ cup rice vinegar
½ cup packed light brown sugar
1 tablespoon cornstarch
1 teaspoon minced ginger
¼ teaspoon garlic powder
1 pound boneless, skinless chicken breasts

GINGER PASTE

If you struggle with mincing your own ginger, look for ginger paste in your local grocery store. The cost per teaspoon is just pennies more than fresh, and it saves a lot of time. It comes in a clear plastic tube and can often be found in the produce section. Ginger paste can be stored in the refrigerator for several months after opening.

1 In a small bowl, whisk together soy sauce, rice vinegar, brown sugar, cornstarch, ginger, and garlic powder.

2 Place chicken and sauce into Instant Pot®. Stir to combine.

3 Close lid and set pressure release to Sealing.

4 Press Manual or Pressure Cook button and adjust time to 15 minutes.

5 When the timer beeps, allow pressure to release naturally and then unlock lid and remove it.

6 Serve.

PER SERVING

CALORIES: 259 | FAT: 3g | PROTEIN: 28g | SODIUM: 1,809mg
FIBER: 0g | CARBOHYDRATES: 29g | SUGAR: 25g

Chicken Potato Casserole

This creamy casserole is hearty and filling—thanks to the potatoes mixed in with the chicken.

- **Total Recipe Cost:** $4.68
- **Hands-On Time:** 10 minutes
- **Cook Time:** 15 minutes

Serves 4

3 medium russet potatoes, peeled and chopped

1 pound boneless, skinless chicken thighs

4 tablespoons unsalted butter

4 tablespoons all-purpose flour

½ teaspoon salt

¼ teaspoon black pepper

1 cup heavy whipping cream

1 cup shredded Cheddar cheese

1 cup water

1 Place potatoes and chicken in a 6-cup metal bowl. Mix.

2 Press Sauté button and place butter into Instant Pot®.

3 Once butter is melted, whisk in flour. Continue to whisk until fully combined and flour is browned, 2 minutes.

4 Season with salt and pepper and mix an additional 30 seconds.

5 Slowly whisk in cream. Continue to whisk 2 minutes until sauce is thickened and no longer lumpy.

6 Pour sauce over chicken and potatoes. Top with Cheddar cheese. Spray a piece of foil with cooking spray and tightly cover top of bowl with foil.

7 Clean inner pot and place back inside Instant Pot® and pour in water. Place trivet inside Instant Pot®. Create a foil sling and carefully lower bowl into Instant Pot®.

8 Close lid and set pressure release to Sealing.

9 Press Manual or Pressure Cook button and adjust time to 10 minutes.

10 When the timer beeps, allow pressure to release naturally and then unlock lid and remove it. Remove pan from Instant Pot® using foil sling and then remove foil from top of bowl. Serve.

PER SERVING

CALORIES: 694 | FAT: 47g | PROTEIN: 34g | SODIUM: 607mg
FIBER: 3g | CARBOHYDRATES: 34g | SUGAR: 3g

Honey Garlic Chicken

This sweet and sticky chicken tastes great paired with a steamed vegetable like green beans or carrots.

- **Total Recipe Cost: $3.12**
- **Hands-On Time: 5 minutes**
- **Cook Time: 17 minutes**

Serves 4

1 pound boneless, skinless chicken thighs
¼ teaspoon salt
⅛ teaspoon black pepper
1 tablespoon olive oil
1 cup chicken broth
⅓ cup honey
6 cloves garlic, minced
2 tablespoons rice vinegar
1 tablespoon soy sauce
1 tablespoon cornstarch
½ cup cold water

1 Season chicken with salt and pepper.

2 Press Sauté button and add oil to the Instant Pot®.

3 Place chicken in pot and let brown 30 seconds on each side.

4 Remove chicken and pour broth into pot to deglaze. Turn Instant Pot® off.

5 In a small bowl, whisk together honey, garlic, vinegar, and soy sauce.

6 Place chicken back in Instant Pot® and pour sauce on top.

7 Close lid and set pressure release to Sealing.

8 Press Manual or Pressure Cook button and adjust time to 10 minutes.

9 When the timer beeps, allow pressure to release naturally for 10 minutes and then quick release remaining pressure. Unlock lid and remove it.

10 Remove chicken and set aside.

11 Press Sauté button.

12 In a small bowl, whisk together cornstarch and water. Mix cornstarch slurry into sauce in pot and bring to a boil. Let sauce boil 5 minutes.

13 Serve sauce over chicken.

PER SERVING

CALORIES: 276 | FAT: 8g | PROTEIN: 24g | SODIUM: 497mg
FIBER: 0g | CARBOHYDRATES: 27g | SUGAR: 23g

Cheesy Chicken and Rice

This classic dish saves time in the Instant Pot® because the chicken and rice cook quickly—and all in one pot.

- **Total Recipe Cost: $3.68**
- **Hands-On Time:** 5 minutes
- **Cook Time:** 16 minutes

Serves 4

3 tablespoons olive oil
1 pound boneless, skinless chicken thighs, cut into 1" pieces
1 cup white rice
½ teaspoon salt
¼ teaspoon black pepper
1½ cups chicken broth
1 cup shredded Cheddar cheese

1 Press Sauté button and add oil to the Instant Pot®.

2 Add chicken and rice. Season with salt and pepper. Let cook 5 minutes.

3 Pour in broth and deglaze bottom of pot.

4 Close lid and set pressure release to Sealing.

5 Press Manual or Pressure Cook button and adjust time to 10 minutes.

6 When the timer beeps, allow pressure to release naturally and then unlock lid and remove it.

7 Mix in cheese and serve.

PER SERVING

CALORIES: 520 | FAT: 25g | PROTEIN: 34g | SODIUM: 619mg
FIBER: 1g | CARBOHYDRATES: 39g | SUGAR: 0g

Chicken Fajitas

This easy "dump and press start" recipe is a family favorite. The chicken broth creates a wonderful taco sauce that can be drizzled on top of the fajitas before serving.

- **Total Recipe Cost: $7.15**
- **Hands-On Time:** 10 minutes
- **Cook Time:** 12 minutes

Serves 6

1 pound boneless, skinless chicken thighs, sliced

1 cup chicken broth

1 medium sweet onion, peeled and sliced

1 medium red bell pepper, seeded and sliced

1 medium green bell pepper, seeded and sliced

1 (4-ounce) can mild diced green chilies

1 (1-ounce) packet taco seasoning

2 tablespoons lime juice

6 (10") flour tortillas, warmed

1 Combine all ingredients except tortillas in the Instant Pot®. Stir to combine.

2 Close lid and set pressure release to Sealing.

3 Press Manual or Pressure Cook button and adjust time to 12 minutes.

4 When the timer beeps, allow pressure to release naturally and then unlock lid and remove it.

5 Serve in warmed flour tortillas.

PER SERVING

CALORIES: 350 | FAT: 9g | PROTEIN: 23g | SODIUM: 1,053mg
FIBER: 5g | CARBOHYDRATES: 44g | SUGAR: 7g

Chicken Alfredo

This tasty Chicken Alfredo tastes like it came from a fancy restaurant, but for a lot less money and not much hands-on time.

- **Total Recipe Cost:** $7.81
- **Hands-On Time:** 10 minutes
- **Cook Time:** 13 minutes

Serves 6

2 tablespoons olive oil
1 pound boneless, skinless chicken breasts, sliced
1 teaspoon garlic salt
½ teaspoon black pepper
4 cups chicken broth
1 pound fettuccine
8 tablespoons butter, cubed
1 cup heavy whipping cream
1 cup grated Parmesan cheese

FREEZING CREAMY PASTA DISHES

Creamy pasta dishes freeze surprisingly well. Let the pasta fully cool and then store in the freezer in a gallon-sized zip-top bag up to three months. When ready to serve, defrost overnight in the refrigerator and reheat in the microwave or stovetop with a couple of tablespoons of milk.

1. Press Sauté button on Instant Pot® and add oil.

2. Place chicken in pot and season with garlic salt and pepper. Let cook, stirring occasionally, 7 minutes.

3. Pour in broth and deglaze bottom of pot.

4. Break fettuccine in half and place in pot. Top fettuccine with butter.

5. Close lid and set pressure release to Sealing.

6. Press Manual or Pressure Cook button and adjust time to 6 minutes.

7. When the timer beeps, quick release pressure and then unlock lid and remove it.

8. Pour in cream and Parmesan and mix until fully combined.

9. Serve hot.

PER SERVING

CALORIES: 767 | FAT: 42g | PROTEIN: 37g | SODIUM: 662mg
FIBER: 4g | CARBOHYDRATES: 60g | SUGAR: 3g

Pesto Chicken

This flavorful and easy chicken dinner is perfect for a busy weeknight because it takes mere minutes to make.

- **Total Recipe Cost: $3.77**
- **Hands-On Time: 5 minutes**
- **Cook Time: 15 minutes**

Serves 4

1 cup water
1 pound boneless, skinless chicken breasts, cut into strips
½ cup pesto
2 Roma tomatoes, sliced
¼ teaspoon salt
⅛ teaspoon black pepper

1 Pour water into Instant Pot® and add trivet.

2 In a 6-cup metal bowl, combine chicken, pesto, tomatoes, salt, and pepper.

3 Create a foil sling and carefully lower bowl into Instant Pot®.

4 Close lid and set pressure release to Sealing.

5 Press Manual or Pressure Cook button and adjust time to 15 minutes.

6 When the timer beeps, allow pressure to release naturally and then unlock lid and remove it. Remove pan from Instant Pot® using foil sling.

7 Serve hot.

PER SERVING

CALORIES: 272 | FAT: 16g | PROTEIN: 27g | SODIUM: 502mg
FIBER: 1g | CARBOHYDRATES: 3g | SUGAR: 1g

Sour Cream Enchiladas

These creamy enchiladas are perfect for those days when you have leftover chicken. Instead of eating the same thing two nights in a row, repurpose your leftovers into a new delicious meal.

- **Total Recipe Cost:** $5.62
- **Hands-On Time:** 10 minutes
- **Cook Time:** 12 minutes

Serves 4

2 tablespoons butter

2 tablespoons all-purpose flour

1 cup chicken broth

1 cup full-fat sour cream

1 (4-ounce) can mild diced green chilies, divided

1 cup water

1½ cups shredded cooked chicken

1½ cups shredded Monterey jack cheese

4 (8") flour tortillas

1 Press Sauté button on Instant Pot® and add butter. Let butter melt and then whisk in flour. Continue to whisk butter and flour until flour is browned and sauce is smooth, about 2 minutes.

2 Slowly whisk in broth. Cook 2 minutes, stirring constantly.

3 Remove sauce from Instant Pot® and let cool in a separate bowl for 5 minutes.

4 Mix sour cream and half the canned diced chilies into sauce and set aside.

5 Wash Instant Pot® and pour in 1 cup water. Add a trivet to Instant Pot®.

6 Divide chicken, cheese, and remaining half-can diced chilies among four tortillas.

7 Roll tortillas up and arrange side by side in a 7" cake pan. Pour sauce over rolled-up tortillas. Tightly cover cake pan with foil.

8 Create a foil sling and slowly lower enchiladas into Instant Pot®.

9 Close lid and set pressure release to Sealing.

10 Press Manual or Pressure Cook button and adjust time to 5 minutes.

11 When the timer beeps, quick release pressure and then unlock lid and remove it.

12 Remove cake pan using foil sling, unwrap foil from top of pan, and serve hot.

PER SERVING

CALORIES: 567 | FAT: 33g | PROTEIN: 35g | SODIUM: 645mg
FIBER: 2g | CARBOHYDRATES: 32g | SUGAR: 3g

Cajun Chicken Pasta

This restaurant copycat dish is creamy and spicy and perfectly filling thanks to the hearty noodles and chicken.

- **Total Recipe Cost:** $7.82
- **Hands-On Time:** 10 minutes
- **Cook Time:** 13 minutes

Serves 6

2 tablespoons olive oil
1 pound boneless, skinless chicken breasts, sliced
1 tablespoon Cajun seasoning
4 cups chicken broth
1 pound penne pasta
8 tablespoons butter, cubed
1 cup heavy whipping cream
1 cup grated Parmesan cheese

TONING DOWN THE SPICE
If you are looking for the Cajun flavors with less heat, try switching out the Cajun seasoning for creole seasoning. It still gives you that same flavor without the heat.

1 Press Sauté button on Instant Pot® and add oil.

2 Place chicken in Instant Pot® and sprinkle with Cajun seasoning. Let cook, stirring occasionally, 7 minutes.

3 Pour in broth and deglaze bottom of pot.

4 Place pasta in pot. Top pasta and chicken with butter.

5 Close lid and set pressure release to Sealing.

6 Press Manual or Pressure Cook button and adjust time to 5 minutes.

7 When the timer beeps, quick release pressure and then unlock lid and remove it.

8 Pour in cream and Parmesan and mix until fully combined.

9 Serve hot.

PER SERVING

CALORIES: 767 | **FAT:** 42g | **PROTEIN:** 37g | **SODIUM:** 400mg
FIBER: 4g | **CARBOHYDRATES:** 60g | **SUGAR:** 3g

Chicken Stir-Fry

Chicken Stir-Fry is extremely versatile. This recipe calls for broccoli, red pepper, and cucumber but you could easily switch them out for other vegetables like cauliflower, carrots, bok choy, or zucchini. Use whatever is in season for the best flavors.

- **Total Recipe Cost:** $7.35
- **Hands-On Time:** 10 minutes
- **Cook Time:** 18 minutes

Serves 4

2 tablespoons olive oil

1 pound boneless, skinless chicken breasts, cut into 1" pieces

½ teaspoon salt

¼ teaspoon black pepper

1 medium bunch broccoli, cut into small florets

1 medium cucumber, sliced and halved

1 medium red bell pepper, seeded and sliced

1 tablespoon minced ginger

2 cloves garlic, minced

½ cup stir-fry sauce

2 cups cooked brown rice, warmed

1 Press Sauté button on Instant Pot®. Add oil to Instant Pot® and let heat 1 minute.

2 Add chicken, salt, and pepper to Instant Pot®. Cover and let cook until no longer pink inside, about 8 minutes, stirring occasionally. Remove chicken from Instant Pot® and set aside.

3 Add broccoli, cucumber, bell pepper, and ginger to Instant Pot®. Stir-fry until vegetables are tender, about 5 minutes.

4 Add garlic and cook an additional 30 seconds.

5 Add chicken back to Instant Pot® and pour in stir-fry sauce. Mix to coat with sauce. Bring sauce to a boil and let cook 2 minutes.

6 Remove from heat and serve over rice.

PER SERVING

CALORIES: 426 | FAT: 11g | PROTEIN: 35g | SODIUM: 1,437mg
FIBER: 7g | CARBOHYDRATES: 48g | SUGAR: 11g

Pulled Chicken Sandwiches

Pulled Chicken Sandwiches are sweet and tender meat served on a bun or soft roll. The quick cook time makes them a perfectly easy weeknight meal.

- **Total Recipe Cost: $3.79**
- **Hands-On Time: 10 minutes**
- **Cook Time: 15 minutes**

Serves 4

1 pound boneless, skinless chicken breasts
¼ teaspoon salt
⅛ teaspoon black pepper
1½ cups barbecue sauce, divided
1 cup water
4 hamburger buns

WANT IT CRISPIER?

If you are looking for that crispy texture you sometimes find with pulled meats, simply spread the cooked pulled chicken in a thin layer on a large baking pan. Then, place it under the broiler for 1–2 minutes, just until the top of the chicken starts to crisp up. Don't leave it too long or it will dry out.

1 Place chicken in a 6-cup metal bowl. Season chicken with salt and pepper and brush with 1 cup barbecue sauce.

2 Pour water in Instant Pot®. Add trivet to Instant Pot®.

3 Create a foil sling and carefully lower bowl of chicken into Instant Pot®.

4 Close lid and set pressure release to Sealing.

5 Press Manual or Pressure Cook button and adjust time to 15 minutes.

6 When the timer beeps, allow pressure to release naturally for 10 minutes, then quick release remaining pressure. Unlock lid and remove it.

7 Use foil sling to remove the bowl of chicken.

8 Drain any water in bowl and shred chicken with two forks.

9 Add remaining ½ cup barbecue sauce and stir to combine.

10 Serve pulled chicken on warmed hamburger buns.

PER SERVING

CALORIES: 434 | FAT: 5g | PROTEIN: 31g | SODIUM: 1,461mg
FIBER: 2g | CARBOHYDRATES: 64g | SUGAR: 37g

8

Beef and Pork Main Dishes

There are so many great recipes you can make in your Instant Pot® with beef and pork as the star. To save money on these recipes, make sure you check your weekly grocery flyers for deals before buying meat. Buying ground beef in bulk is also a great option. It is often cheaper when bought in bulk and can be stored in the freezer for many months.

Red Beans and Rice

A yummy pot-in-pot recipe made with flavorful andouille sausage, red kidney beans, and fluffy white rice. Do you want to add more heat to this recipe? Add ½ teaspoon of cayenne pepper to the red beans and switch the creole seasoning to Cajun seasoning for extra spice.

- **Total Recipe Cost:** $8.23
- **Hands-On Time:** 10 minutes
- **Cook Time:** 28 minutes

Serves 4

2 tablespoons olive oil

1 large yellow onion, peeled and chopped

4 cloves garlic, minced

3 cups water, divided

2 (15.5-ounce) cans red kidney beans, drained and rinsed

1 medium green bell pepper, seeded and chopped

1 (13.5-ounce) package andouille smoked sausage

1 tablespoon creole seasoning

1 teaspoon hot sauce

2 bay leaves

2 cups white rice, rinsed well

⅛ teaspoon salt

1 Set Instant Pot® to Sauté and heat oil. Once the oil is hot, add onion and sauté until soft, about 7 minutes.

2 Add garlic and cook until fragrant, about 30 seconds.

3 Pour in 1 cup water and deglaze bottom of pot. Turn Instant Pot® off.

4 Add beans, bell pepper, sausage, creole seasoning, hot sauce, and bay leaves to Instant Pot®. Stir to combine.

5 Place trivet inside Instant Pot®, on top of bean mixture.

6 In a 6-cup metal bowl, mix together rice, remaining 2 cups water, and salt.

7 Create foil sling and lower bowl of rice on top of trivet.

8 Close lid and set pressure release to Sealing.

9 Press Manual or Pressure Cook button and adjust time to 20 minutes.

10 When the timer beeps, quick release pressure and then unlock lid and remove it.

11 Remove bowl of rice using foil sling and fluff with a fork.

12 Remove bay leaves from beans and serve beans hot over cooked rice.

PER SERVING

CALORIES: 770 | FAT: 21g | PROTEIN: 35g | SODIUM: 1,387mg
FIBER: 10g | CARBOHYDRATES: 110g | SUGAR: 9g

Tamale Pie

This classic casserole dish is beef tamale filling on the inside with a corn bread–style topping.

- **Total Recipe Cost: $7.68**
- **Hands-On Time:** 15 minutes
- **Cook Time:** 35 minutes

Serves 4

1 cup water

1 pound ground beef

½ medium yellow onion, peeled and diced

1 medium green bell pepper, seeded and diced

½ cup frozen corn kernels, thawed

1 (2.25-ounce) can sliced black olives

1 (4-ounce) can mild diced green chilies

1 (1-ounce) packet taco seasoning

¾ cup corn masa

½ teaspoon baking soda

½ teaspoon salt

1 (15-ounce) can creamed corn

¼ cup vegetable oil

¼ cup grated Mexican-blend cheese

1 Put water inside Instant Pot® and add trivet.

2 In a 7" cake pan, combine ground beef, onion, bell pepper, corn kernels, olives, green chilies, and taco seasoning. Set aside.

3 In a medium bowl, mix together corn masa, baking soda, and salt.

4 Make a well in center of mixture and pour in creamed corn, oil, and cheese. Mix just until combined, batter will still be lumpy. Pour corn bread batter over meat mixture.

5 Cover cake pan tightly with foil. Create a foil sling and lower pan into Instant Pot®.

6 Close lid and set pressure release to Sealing.

7 Press Manual or Pressure Cook button and adjust time to 35 minutes.

8 When the timer beeps, quick release pressure and then unlock lid and remove it.

9 Remove cake pan using foil sling. Let sit 5 minutes and then serve.

PER SERVING

CALORIES: 659 | FAT: 36g | PROTEIN: 30g | SODIUM: 1,624mg
FIBER: 6g | CARBOHYDRATES: 59g | SUGAR: 13g

Taco-Stuffed Peppers

This fun spin on stuffed peppers tastes great and is a healthier way to celebrate taco night.

- **Total Recipe Cost: $7.97**
- **Hands-On Time: 10 minutes**
- **Cook Time: 8 minutes**

Serves 4

1 cup water
1 pound ground beef
1 (1-ounce) packet taco
   seasoning
1 (4-ounce) can mild diced
   green chilies
1 cup cooked rice
4 large bell peppers
½ cup grated Monterey jack
   cheese

WHICH BELL PEPPER VARIETY SHOULD YOU CHOOSE?

The color bell pepper you choose for stuffed peppers is a personal preference. Many people like to serve them in a variety of colors because it's pretty. Keep in mind that red bell peppers are sweeter than green bell peppers, but green bell peppers cost about 50 percent less. The total recipe cost is based on green bell peppers.

1 Pour water into Instant Pot® and add trivet.

2 In a medium bowl, mix together ground beef, taco seasoning, green chilies, and cooked rice. Set aside.

3 Slice tops of bell peppers off and remove seeds from inside peppers.

4 Scoop ground beef mixture into each pepper and fill just to the top.

5 Carefully place stuffed peppers inside Instant Pot® so they are standing upright on trivet.

6 Close lid and set pressure release to Sealing.

7 Press Manual or Pressure Cook button and adjust time to 8 minutes.

8 When the timer beeps, quick release pressure and then unlock lid and remove it.

9 Remove peppers and sprinkle them with cheese and serve hot.

PER SERVING

CALORIES: 481 | **FAT:** 22g | **PROTEIN:** 28g | **SODIUM:** 818mg
FIBER: 5g | **CARBOHYDRATES:** 26g | **SUGAR:** 9g

Cajun Sausage and Potatoes

Cajun Sausage and Potatoes makes a great dish to bring to a potluck. If you have access to an electrical outlet, bring the cooked dish in your Instant Pot® and press the Keep Warm button. This will keep it warm and ready to eat for the duration of the party.

- **Total Recipe Cost: $6.68**
- **Hands-On Time: 10 minutes**
- **Cook Time: 10 minutes**

Serves 6

2½ pounds red potatoes, chopped

1 (13.5-ounce) package andouille smoked sausage, sliced

1 medium sweet onion, peeled and chopped

1 (10.5-ounce) can cream of mushroom soup

1 teaspoon Cajun seasoning

1 cup beef broth

1 Place potatoes, sausage, and onion in Instant Pot®.

2 In a small bowl, whisk together cream of mushroom soup, Cajun seasoning, and broth. Pour sauce over potatoes and stir.

3 Close lid and set pressure release to Sealing.

4 Press Manual or Pressure Cook button and adjust time to 10 minutes.

5 When the timer beeps, quick release pressure and then unlock lid and remove it.

6 Serve hot.

PER SERVING

CALORIES: 294 | FAT: 10g | PROTEIN: 17g | SODIUM: 883mg
FIBER: 4g | CARBOHYDRATES: 35g | SUGAR: 5g

Mongolian Beef

Enjoy the flavors of Mongolian Beef while staying within your budget. This dish is packed with flavor but uses a less expensive cut of meat to keep costs down.

- **Total Recipe Cost:** $3.77
- **Hands-On Time:** 10 minutes
- **Cook Time:** 8 minutes

Serves 4

1 tablespoon olive oil

1 pound ground beef

½ cup soy sauce

½ cup packed light brown sugar

½ cup water

1 teaspoon minced ginger

⅛ teaspoon red pepper flakes

1 tablespoon all-purpose flour

½ teaspoon salt

½ teaspoon black pepper

3 tablespoons sliced green onions

2 cups cooked brown rice, warmed

1 Press Sauté button on Instant Pot® and add oil. Add ground beef and cook, stirring occasionally, 5 minutes.

2 While beef is cooking, mix soy sauce, brown sugar, water, ginger, and red pepper flakes in a small bowl.

3 Drain fat from Instant Pot®.

4 Sprinkle ground beef with flour, salt, and black pepper. Mix and cook an additional 30 seconds.

5 Pour sauce over beef and deglaze bottom of pot. Turn Instant Pot® off.

6 Close lid and set pressure release to Sealing.

7 Press Manual or Pressure Cook button and adjust time to 2 minutes.

8 When the timer beeps, allow pressure to release naturally for 10 minutes and then quick release remaining pressure. Unlock lid and remove it.

9 Sprinkle beef with green onions and serve over rice.

PER SERVING

CALORIES: 515 | **FAT:** 21g | **PROTEIN:** 26g | **SODIUM:** 2,133mg
FIBER: 2g | **CARBOHYDRATES:** 54g | **SUGAR:** 27g

Hamburger Stroganoff

Hamburger Stroganoff is a frugal version of traditional beef stroganoff. You save money by using ground beef in place of steak, but don't have to sacrifice on the flavorful, creamy sauce.

- **Total Recipe Cost:** $9.23
- **Hands-On Time:** 10 minutes
- **Cook Time:** 9 minutes

Serves 4

1 tablespoon olive oil
½ medium yellow onion, peeled and diced
1 pound ground beef
2 tablespoons all-purpose flour
½ teaspoon salt
¼ teaspoon black pepper
2 cloves garlic, minced
3 cups beef broth
1 cup sliced mushrooms
1 tablespoon tomato paste
3 cups wide egg noodles
1 cup full-fat sour cream
½ cup cold water
1 tablespoon cornstarch

TRADITIONAL BEEF STROGANOFF

Beef stroganoff is traditionally made with strips of beef. If you can find flank steak on sale, then you could substitute it for the ground beef. Simply sear it in the Instant Pot® for 1–2 minutes as opposed to browning for 4 minutes. Then follow the rest of the instructions as listed.

1 Press Sauté button on Instant Pot® and add oil and onion. Add ground beef and let cook 4 minutes, stirring occasionally.

2 Sprinkle beef with flour, salt, and pepper. Stir. Add garlic and cook an additional 30 seconds.

3 Drain fat from ground beef.

4 Pour in broth and deglaze bottom of pot. Turn Instant Pot® off.

5 Add mushrooms and tomato paste. Stir to combine. Place egg noodles in Instant Pot®.

6 Close lid and set pressure release to Sealing.

7 Press Manual or Pressure Cook button and adjust time to 4 minutes.

8 When the timer beeps, quick release pressure and then unlock lid and remove it.

9 Mix in sour cream.

10 In a small bowl, whisk together water and cornstarch. Pour cornstarch slurry into stroganoff and stir until fully incorporated.

11 Serve hot.

PER SERVING

CALORIES: 523 | FAT: 31g | PROTEIN: 30g | SODIUM: 1,060mg
FIBER: 1g | CARBOHYDRATES: 29g | SUGAR: 3g

Mini Meatloaves

This a fun twist on traditional meatloaf. This recipe uses a Bundt pan to keep the Mini Meatloaves in place while cooking. They are really fun when served with mashed potatoes on top as frosting.

- **Total Recipe Cost: $3.26**
- **Hands-On Time:** 15 minutes
- **Cook Time:** 35 minutes

Serves 6

1 cup water
1 pound ground beef
1 large egg
½ cup bread crumbs
¼ cup ketchup
2 tablespoons onion powder
1 tablespoon Worcestershire sauce
1 teaspoon salt
¼ teaspoon black pepper

1. Pour water into Instant Pot® and add trivet.

2. In a medium bowl, combine beef, egg, bread crumbs, ketchup, onion powder, Worcestershire, salt, and pepper and mix well.

3. Scoop meatloaf mixture into six silicone muffin cups. Arrange muffin cups around a 6-cup Bundt pan. Cover Bundt pan with foil.

4. Create a foil sling and carefully lower pan into Instant Pot®.

5. Close lid and set pressure release to Sealing.

6. Press Manual or Pressure Cook button and adjust time to 35 minutes.

7. When the timer beeps, allow pressure to release naturally and then unlock lid and remove it.

8. Remove Bundt pan using foil sling. Serve meatloaf muffins hot.

PER SERVING

CALORIES: 232 | FAT: 13g | PROTEIN: 17g | SODIUM: 648mg
FIBER: 1g | CARBOHYDRATES: 12g | SUGAR: 3g

Taco Casserole

Taco Casserole is nachos in reverse. It's taco meat cooked in beef gravy and topped with chips and cheese. Then it's cooked in a casserole and transformed into a hearty and tasty dinner.

- **Total Recipe Cost: $5.87**
- **Hands-On Time: 10 minutes**
- **Cook Time: 17 minutes**

Serves 4

1 pound ground beef
⅛ cup all-purpose flour
1 (1-ounce) packet taco
    seasoning
1 cup beef broth
2 cups tortilla chips
1 cup shredded Cheddar
    cheese
1 cup water
½ cup full-fat sour cream

1 Press Sauté button on Instant Pot®. Add beef to pot and cook, stirring occasionally, 5 minutes. Drain fat from ground beef.

2 Sprinkle beef with flour and taco seasoning. Pour in broth and mix.

3 Bring to a boil and let cook 5 minutes until sauce is thickened, stirring occasionally. Turn Instant Pot® off.

4 Scoop half of meat mixture into a 7" cake pan. Spread 1 cup chips over meat. Top chips with ½ cup cheese. Repeat with remaining meat, chips, and cheese. Cover pan with foil.

5 Clean inner pot and place back inside Instant Pot®. Pour water into Instant Pot® and add trivet.

6 Create a foil sling and carefully lower pan into Instant Pot®.

7 Close lid and set pressure release to Sealing.

8 Press Manual or Pressure Cook button and adjust time to 7 minutes.

9 When the timer beeps, allow pressure to release naturally for 10 minutes, then quick release remaining pressure. Unlock lid and remove it.

10 Remove cake pan using foil sling and serve with sour cream as garnish.

PER SERVING

CALORIES: 508 | **FAT:** 34g | **PROTEIN:** 30g | **SODIUM:** 1,106mg
FIBER: 2g | **CARBOHYDRATES:** 19g | **SUGAR:** 2g

Ranch Pork Chops

These tasty pork chops cook fast and stay moist in the Instant Pot®.

- **Total Recipe Cost: $5.70**
- **Hands-On Time: 5 minutes**
- **Cook Time: 7 minutes**

Serves 4

2 tablespoons olive oil

1 pound thick-cut boneless
   pork chops

½ teaspoon salt

¼ teaspoon black pepper

1 cup chicken broth

1 (1-ounce) ranch seasoning
   packet

1 Press Sauté button on Instant Pot® and add oil. Let oil heat up 1 minute.

2 Add pork chops in a single layer and sprinkle with salt and pepper. Let cook 30 seconds and flip. Cook an additional 30 seconds.

3 In a small bowl, whisk together chicken broth and ranch seasoning. Pour in broth mixture and deglaze bottom of pot.

4 Turn Instant Pot® off.

5 Close lid and set pressure release to Sealing.

6 Press Manual or Pressure Cook button and adjust time to 5 minutes.

7 When the timer beeps, allow pressure to release naturally and then unlock lid and remove it.

8 Serve hot.

PER SERVING

CALORIES: 219 | **FAT:** 14g | **PROTEIN:** 21g | **SODIUM:** 742mg
FIBER: 0g | **CARBOHYDRATES:** 10g | **SUGAR:** 0g

Asian Lettuce Wraps

This sweet and healthy dinner is made with ground pork and a flavor-filled Asian sauce. If you cannot find bib lettuce at your local grocer then butter lettuce may be used.

- **Total Recipe Cost: $10.27**
- **Hands-On Time: 10 minutes**
- **Cook Time: 8 minutes**

Serves 4

2 tablespoons olive oil
1 pound ground pork
2 medium carrots, diced
1 medium bunch green
    onions, sliced
½ cup water
1 cup hoisin sauce
1 cup soy sauce
2 teaspoons minced ginger
½ teaspoon red pepper flakes
1 (8-ounce) can water
    chestnuts, drained
1 small head bib lettuce

WHAT IS HOISIN SAUCE?

Hoisin sauce is a popular Asian sauce made with soy beans, sweet potato, sesame seeds, garlic, and chili pepper. It's dark red hue and sweetness add a lot of color and flavor to this dish.

1. Press Sauté button on Instant Pot®. Add oil, ground pork, carrots, and green onions to Instant Pot®. Cook, stirring occasionally, 5 minutes.

2. Pour in water and deglaze bottom of pot. Turn Instant Pot® off.

3. In a small bowl, mix hoisin sauce, soy sauce, ginger, and red pepper flakes together. Pour sauce and water chestnuts over pork. Do not stir.

4. Close lid and set pressure release to Sealing.

5. Press Manual or Pressure Cook button and adjust time to 2 minutes.

6. When the timer beeps, allow pressure to release naturally and then unlock lid and remove it.

7. Mix ingredients together. Scoop pork into bib lettuce leaves and serve.

PER SERVING

CALORIES: 533 | FAT: 26g | PROTEIN: 30g | SODIUM: 4,642mg
FIBER: 6g | CARBOHYDRATES: 45g | SUGAR: 22g

Pork Chops with Cinnamon Apples

Have your dessert and eat it too! These cinnamon apples are sweet enough to be eaten as dessert but taste wonderful when paired with tender pork chops.

- **Total Recipe Cost: $7.62**
- **Hands-On Time: 15 minutes**
- **Cook Time: 7 minutes**

Serves 4

2 tablespoons olive oil
1 pound thick-cut boneless
    pork chops
½ teaspoon salt
¼ teaspoon black pepper
1 cup chicken broth
3 medium Gala apples,
    peeled and sliced
4 tablespoons brown sugar
1 tablespoon lemon juice
1 teaspoon ground cinnamon
¼ teaspoon ground nutmeg

1 Press Sauté button on Instant Pot® and add oil. Let oil heat up 1 minute.

2 Add pork chops in a single layer and sprinkle with salt and pepper. Let cook 30 seconds and flip. Cook an additional 30 seconds.

3 Pour in broth and deglaze bottom of pot.

4 Turn Instant Pot® off.

5 In a 6-cup metal bowl, combine apples, brown sugar, lemon juice, cinnamon, and nutmeg. Cover bowl with foil.

6 Place trivet inside Instant Pot®, over pork chops.

7 Create a foil sling and carefully lower bowl into Instant Pot®.

8 Close lid and set pressure release to Sealing.

9 Press Manual or Pressure Cook button and adjust time to 5 minutes.

10 When the timer beeps, allow pressure to release naturally and then unlock lid and remove it.

11 Remove bowl of apples from Instant Pot® using foil sling and then remove pork chops. Serve together.

PER SERVING

CALORIES: 333 | **FAT:** 14g | **PROTEIN:** 22g | **SODIUM:** 347mg
FIBER: 2g | **CARBOHYDRATES:** 30g | **SUGAR:** 26g

Beef and Broccoli Casserole

This casserole, sometimes referred to as "poor man's casserole," is a hearty dish filled with ground beef, potatoes, and broccoli.

- **Total Recipe Cost: $6.60**
- **Hands-On Time: 15 minutes**
- **Cook Time: 25 minutes**

Serves 4

1 cup water
1 pound ground beef
2 large red potatoes, cut into ¼"-thick slices
1 medium head broccoli, chopped
1 (10.5-ounce) can cream of mushroom soup
½ cup beef broth
1 teaspoon Italian seasoning
½ teaspoon salt
¼ teaspoon black pepper
1 cup shredded Cheddar cheese

1 Pour water into Instant Pot® and add trivet.

2 Spread ground beef on bottom of a 7" cake pan. Arrange sliced potatoes over beef. Sprinkle broccoli over potatoes.

3 In a small bowl, whisk together cream of mushroom soup, broth, Italian seasoning, salt, and pepper. Pour sauce over casserole and top with cheese.

4 Spray a piece of foil with cooking spray and cover cake pan. Create a foil sling and carefully lower pan into Instant Pot®.

5 Close lid and set pressure release to Sealing.

6 Press Manual or Pressure Cook button and adjust time to 25 minutes.

7 When the timer beeps, allow pressure to release naturally and then unlock lid and remove it.

8 Remove cake pan from Instant Pot® using foil sling. Serve hot.

PER SERVING

CALORIES: 606 | **FAT:** 30g | **PROTEIN:** 38g | **SODIUM:** 994mg
FIBER: 7g | **CARBOHYDRATES:** 49g | **SUGAR:** 6g

Sweet and Spicy Meatloaf

This recipe is made with the perfect combination of Italian sausage and ground beef. The vegetables add a delicious layer of flavor and texture that you are sure to enjoy.

- **Total Recipe Cost:** $8.59
- **Hands-On Time:** 15 minutes
- **Cook Time:** 46 minutes

Serves 6

2 tablespoons olive oil
3 medium carrots, diced
1 small red onion, peeled and diced
4 cloves garlic, minced
⅔ cup ketchup, divided
2 tablespoons Worcestershire sauce
1 cup water
1 pound ground beef
1 pound mild spicy Italian sausage, casings removed
2 large eggs
½ cup bread crumbs
1 teaspoon black pepper
1 teaspoon crushed red pepper
½ teaspoon salt
½ teaspoon dried parsley

COOKING MEATLOAF POT-IN-POT WITH POTATOES

Make this a complete meal by adding 2 pounds of baby potatoes and a small bag of baby carrots to the bottom of the Instant Pot®. Pour 1 cup chicken broth (in place of the water) over the vegetables and let them cook at the same time as the meatloaf.

1 Set Instant Pot® to Sauté and add oil.

2 Add carrots and onion. Cook, stirring occasionally, 5 minutes. Cover and cook another 5 minutes until carrots are tender.

3 Add garlic and cook an additional 30 seconds.

4 Add ⅓ cup ketchup and Worcestershire sauce and stir to combine. Turn Instant Pot® off.

5 Remove cooked vegetables from pot and place in a large bowl.

6 Clean inner pot and put back inside Instant Pot®.

7 Pour water into Instant Pot® and add trivet. Top with steamer basket.

8 To the bowl of cooked vegetables, add ground beef, Italian sausage, eggs, bread crumbs, black pepper, red pepper, salt, and parsley. Mix together with clean hands until fully combined.

9 Shape into a round loaf and place on top of a large piece of foil. Lift the meatloaf with foil and place inside steamer basket within Instant Pot®. Drizzle meatloaf with remaining ⅓ cup ketchup.

10 Close lid and set pressure release to Sealing.

11 Press Manual or Pressure Cook button and adjust time to 35 minutes.

12 When the timer beeps, allow pressure to release naturally and then unlock lid and remove it.

13 Carefully remove meatloaf and drain any fat. Let meatloaf rest 10 minutes before serving.

PER SERVING

CALORIES: 453 | **FAT:** 29g | **PROTEIN:** 26g | **SODIUM:** 972mg
FIBER: 2g | **CARBOHYDRATES:** 23g | **SUGAR:** 10g

Beef and Cheese Burritos

These burritos make an excellent lunch. They are freezer friendly and last several days in the refrigerator if you want to make them ahead of time and eat them all week long. You can reheat leftover burritos in the microwave for 60 seconds.

- **Total Recipe Cost:** $6.39
- **Hands-On Time:** 10 minutes
- **Cook Time:** 15 minutes

Serves 6

1 tablespoon olive oil
½ medium yellow onion, peeled and diced
½ pound ground beef
½ (1-ounce) packet taco seasoning
½ (10-ounce) can red enchilada sauce
½ (16-ounce) can refried beans
6 (10") flour tortillas
2 cups shredded Cheddar cheese

1 Press Sauté button on Instant Pot®. Add oil, onion, and ground beef. Cook, stirring occasionally, 4 minutes.

2 Drain fat from Instant Pot®.

3 Mix in taco seasoning, enchilada sauce, and refried beans. Bring to a boil and let cook 10 minutes until sauce is thickened.

4 Turn Instant Pot® off.

5 Scoop meat mixture into center of each tortilla and top with cheese. Roll each tortilla into a burrito.

6 Eat immediately or store in the refrigerator up to three days.

PER SERVING

CALORIES: 556 | FAT: 29g | PROTEIN: 25g | SODIUM: 1,462mg
FIBER: 7g | CARBOHYDRATES: 48g | SUGAR: 6g

Cheesy Taco Pasta

Cheesy Taco Pasta is packed full of zesty taco flavor, ground beef, and fun shell-shaped pasta, and is topped with melted cheese!

- **Total Recipe Cost: $8.18**
- **Hands-On Time: 5 minutes**
- **Cook Time: 10 minutes**

Serves 4

1 pound ground beef

1 medium yellow onion, peeled and chopped

2 cups beef broth

1 (14.5-ounce) can diced and fire roasted tomatoes

1 (4-ounce) can mild diced green chilies

1 (1-ounce) packet taco seasoning

½ pound small shell-shaped pasta

2 cups grated Mexican-blend cheese

1 Press Sauté button on Instant Pot®. Add ground beef and chopped onion. Cook, stirring occasionally, 5 minutes. Drain fat from pot.

2 Pour in beef broth and deglaze bottom of the pot. Turn Instant Pot® off.

3 Mix in tomatoes, chilies, taco seasoning, and pasta.

4 Close lid and set pressure release to Sealing.

5 Press Manual or Pressure Cook button and adjust time to 4 minutes.

6 When the timer beeps, quick release pressure and then unlock lid and remove it.

7 Mix in cheese before serving.

PER SERVING

CALORIES: 772 | FAT: 38g | PROTEIN: 47g | SODIUM: 2,155mg
FIBER: 6g | CARBOHYDRATES: 59g | SUGAR: 10g

Spaghetti and Meatballs

An easy one-pot Italian dish with delicious homemade meatballs. Although the meatballs are made from scratch, this recipe is still cooked quickly enough to be an easy weeknight dinner.

- **Total Recipe Cost:** $5.55
- **Hands-On Time:** 15 minutes
- **Cook Time:** 5 minutes

Serves 6

1 pound ground beef
¼ cup bread crumbs
¼ cup whole milk
1 tablespoon Worcestershire sauce
1 teaspoon dried basil
½ teaspoon dried parsley
½ teaspoon garlic powder
¾ teaspoon salt
½ teaspoon black pepper
1 pound spaghetti
3 cups water
1 (24-ounce) jar pasta sauce

SAUCE TOO THIN?

If you prefer a thicker sauce, follow these directions after cooking under pressure. Press the Sauté button and bring the sauce to a boil. Let it cook an additional 3–5 minutes until thickened. Don't let it cook too long or your noodles will get mushy.

1 In a large bowl, combine ground beef, bread crumbs, milk, Worcestershire sauce, basil, parsley, garlic powder, salt, and pepper. Mix together with clean hands until fully combined. Form into 1″ meatballs and place at bottom of Instant Pot®.

2 Break spaghetti in half and arrange crisscross on top of meatballs. Pour water over noodles and top with pasta sauce.

3 Close lid and set pressure release to Sealing.

4 Press Manual or Pressure Cook button and adjust time to 5 minutes.

5 When the timer beeps, quick release pressure and then unlock lid and remove it.

6 Mix and serve.

PER SERVING

CALORIES: 537 | **FAT:** 15g | **PROTEIN:** 27g | **SODIUM:** 885mg
FIBER: 6g | **CARBOHYDRATES:** 70g | **SUGAR:** 7g

Goulash

This zesty pasta dish, also sometimes known as American chop suey, is packed with ground beef, bell pepper, tomato, and spices.

- **Total Recipe Cost: $10.59**
- **Hands-On Time: 5 minutes**
- **Cook Time: 12 minutes**

Serves 8

1 tablespoon olive oil
2 pounds ground beef
1 medium yellow onion, peeled and chopped
1 medium green bell pepper, seeded and chopped
¾ teaspoon salt
½ teaspoon black pepper
2 cloves garlic, minced
3 cups water
2 (16-ounce) cans diced tomatoes
1 (8-ounce) can tomato paste
½ teaspoon parsley flakes
½ teaspoon dried oregano
½ teaspoon dried basil
1 bay leaf
1 pound elbow macaroni
1 (24-ounce) jar pasta sauce
1 cup shredded Cheddar cheese

1 Press Sauté button on Instant Pot® and add oil. Add ground beef, onion, bell pepper, salt, and pepper. Cook, stirring occasionally, 5 minutes.

2 Add garlic and cook an additional 30 seconds. Drain fat from pot.

3 Pour in water and deglaze bottom of pot. Turn Instant Pot® off.

4 Add in diced tomatoes, tomato paste, parsley, oregano, basil, and bay leaf.

5 Pour in elbow macaroni and top with pasta sauce. Do not stir.

6 Close lid on Instant Pot® and set pressure release to Sealing.

7 Press Manual or Pressure Cook button and adjust time to 5 minutes.

8 When the timer beeps, quick release pressure and then unlock lid and remove it.

9 Mix and serve immediately, topped with cheese.

PER SERVING

CALORIES: 648 | FAT: 27g | PROTEIN: 37g | SODIUM: 987mg
FIBER: 8g | CARBOHYDRATES: 66g | SUGAR: 15g

"Baked" Ziti

This recipe for "Baked" Ziti is a simple Instant Pot® penne pasta recipe taken to the next level with a creamy and flavorful tomato cheese sauce.

- **Total Recipe Cost: $8.54**
- **Hands-On Time: 5 minutes**
- **Cook Time: 9 minutes**

Serves 6

1 pound ground beef

¾ teaspoon salt

½ teaspoon black pepper

3 cups water

1 pound penne pasta

1½ (24-ounce) jars pasta sauce

1 cup shredded Cheddar cheese

1 cup shredded mozzarella cheese

½ cup grated Parmesan cheese

1 Press Sauté button and add ground beef. Season with salt and pepper. Cook, stirring occasionally, 5 minutes. Drain fat.

2 Pour in water and deglaze bottom of pot. Turn Instant Pot® off.

3 Add in pasta and top with pasta sauce.

4 Close lid and set pressure release to Sealing.

5 Press Manual or Pressure Cook button and adjust time to 4 minutes.

6 When the timer beeps, quick release pressure and then unlock lid and remove it.

7 Stir in Cheddar, mozzarella, and Parmesan cheeses. Serve hot.

PER SERVING

CALORIES: 699 | FAT: 28g | PROTEIN: 38g | SODIUM: 1,447mg
FIBER: 6g | CARBOHYDRATES: 72g | SUGAR: 10g

Seafood and Fish Main Dishes

Cooking seafood in the Instant Pot® is one of those things you don't know you love until you try it. Not only can most cuts of fish cook lightning fast in the Instant Pot®, but they won't get dried out as they do in the oven—thanks to the added water or broth used in every recipe.

Panko-Crusted Tilapia

A simple and delicious fried-fish dish made with Japanese bread crumbs called panko. Try serving this with mashed potatoes and steamed broccoli.

- **Total Recipe Cost:** $5.45
- **Hands-On Time:** 15 minutes
- **Cook Time:** 18 minutes

Serves 4

1 pound tilapia fillets
1 teaspoon salt
½ teaspoon black pepper
1 cup whole milk
3 large eggs, lightly beaten
½ cup panko bread crumbs
6 tablespoons olive oil

HOW IS PANKO DIFFERENT FROM REGULAR BREAD CRUMBS?

Panko bread crumbs are made from crustless bread. It results in an airier bread crumb that makes a crispier crust.

1 Season tilapia with salt and pepper.

2 Set out three bowls; fill one with milk, the second with eggs, and the third with panko.

3 Press Sauté button on Instant Pot® and add oil.

4 Place a tilapia fillet in bowl of milk.

5 Take tilapia from milk bowl and dip in egg. Shake off any excess egg and dip in panko.

6 Place panko-coated tilapia in hot oil.

7 Let cook until golden brown, 3 minutes. Flip and cook an additional 3 minutes. Remove tilapia from Instant Pot® and place on a paper towel–lined plate.

8 Repeat with remaining fish.

9 Let cool slightly before serving.

PER SERVING

CALORIES: 415 | FAT: 28g | PROTEIN: 30g | SODIUM: 446mg
FIBER: 0g | CARBOHYDRATES: 11g | SUGAR: 3g

Tilapia with Pineapple Salsa

Tilapia cooked in a foil packet comes out moist and tender every time. The addition of pineapple salsa adds a wonderful flavor.

- **Total Recipe Cost: $5.36**
- **Hands-On Time: 10 minutes**
- **Cook Time: 2 minutes**

Serves 4

1 pound tilapia fillets
¼ teaspoon salt
⅛ teaspoon black pepper
½ cup pineapple salsa
1 cup water

1 Place tilapia in the center of a 1½' piece of foil. Season tilapia with salt and pepper.

2 Fold foil up on all sides to resemble a bowl and pour in salsa. Fold foil over top of tilapia and crimp edges.

3 Place trivet and water in Instant Pot®. Carefully place foil packet on top of trivet.

4 Close lid and set pressure release to Sealing.

5 Press Manual or Pressure Cook button and adjust time to 2 minutes.

6 When the timer beeps, quick release pressure and then unlock lid and remove it.

7 Remove foil packet from Instant Pot®. Carefully open foil packet; steam will release from inside.

8 Serve tilapia with salsa as garnish.

PER SERVING

CALORIES: 124 | FAT: 2g | PROTEIN: 23g | SODIUM: 294mg
FIBER: 1g | CARBOHYDRATES: 3g | SUGAR: 2g

Tilapia Fish Cakes

A tasty fish cake recipe that will even have fish haters asking for seconds. These fish cakes taste great dipped in sour cream mixed with a little bit of lemon juice!

- **Total Recipe Cost: $5.52**
- **Hands-On Time: 15 minutes**
- **Cook Time: 15 minutes**

Serves 4

½ pound cooked tilapia fillets, shredded

1½ cups bread crumbs, divided

1 cup peeled and shredded russet potato

2 large eggs, lightly beaten

2 tablespoons full-fat sour cream

2 teaspoons lemon juice

1 teaspoon salt

½ teaspoon chili powder

¼ teaspoon black pepper

⅛ teaspoon cayenne pepper

4 tablespoons olive oil

1 In a large bowl, combine tilapia, bread crumbs, potato, eggs, sour cream, lemon juice, salt, chili powder, black pepper, and cayenne pepper. Mix together with clean hands until combined.

2 Press Sauté button on Instant Pot® and add oil.

3 Take golf ball–sized clumps of tilapia mixture. Roll into balls and then flatten to form a cake. Place tilapia cakes in an even layer in Instant Pot®.

4 Cook 2 minutes until golden brown. Flip and cook an additional 2 minutes.

5 Repeat with remaining tilapia mixture.

6 Store tilapia cakes under foil until ready to serve.

PER SERVING

CALORIES: 432 | FAT: 21g | PROTEIN: 24g | SODIUM: 959mg FIBER: 3g | CARBOHYDRATES: 37g | SUGAR: 3g

Tuna Casserole

A classic seafood casserole made with tuna, peas, pasta, and cheese. The flavors in this comfort food dish really meld together when cooked in the Instant Pot®.

- **Total Recipe Cost: $4.41**
- **Hands-On Time: 15 minutes**
- **Cook Time: 30 minutes**

Serves 6

6 tablespoons unsalted butter, divided

4 tablespoons all-purpose flour

½ cup whole milk

1 teaspoon salt

½ teaspoon garlic powder

½ teaspoon onion powder

¼ teaspoon cayenne pepper

1 (12-ounce) can tuna, drained and flaked

½ pound small shell pasta, cooked

½ cup frozen peas, thawed

½ cup shredded Cheddar cheese, divided

¼ cup bread crumbs

1 cup water

1 Press Sauté button on Instant Pot®. Add 4 tablespoons butter to Instant Pot® and melt.

2 Once butter is melted, mix in flour. Stir until flour is golden brown, 2 minutes.

3 Slowly whisk in milk and stir 2 minutes until sauce is thickened and smooth. Season sauce with salt, garlic powder, onion powder, and cayenne.

4 Add in tuna, pasta, peas, and ¼ cup Cheddar cheese. Mix.

5 Turn Instant Pot® off. Pour tuna mixture into a 7" cake pan and top with remaining ¼ cup Cheddar cheese.

6 Cut remaining 2 tablespoons butter into cubes and sprinkle on top of casserole. Top butter with bread crumbs. Cover cake pan tightly with foil.

7 Clean inner pot and place back inside Instant Pot®. Place trivet and water inside Instant Pot®.

8 Create a foil sling and carefully lower cake pan into Instant Pot®.

9 Close lid and set pressure release to Sealing.

10 Press Manual or Pressure Cook button and adjust time to 25 minutes.

11 When the timer beeps, quick release pressure and then unlock lid and remove it.

12 Remove cake pan using foil sling. Serve hot.

PER SERVING

CALORIES: 583 | FAT: 30g | PROTEIN: 33g | SODIUM: 915mg
FIBER: 4g | CARBOHYDRATES: 45g | SUGAR: 4g

Shrimp Spaghetti

A buttery spaghetti dish topped with tender shrimp. This yummy meal tastes like the restaurant variety but costs way less to prepare on your own and is surprisingly easy to make.

- **Total Recipe Cost:** $10.30
- **Hands-On Time:** 5 minutes
- **Cook Time:** 10 minutes

Serves 4

6 tablespoons butter, divided

12 ounces small shrimp, peeled and deveined

½ teaspoon salt

4 cups chicken broth

1 pound spaghetti

1 cup heavy whipping cream

1 cup grated Parmesan cheese

1 teaspoon lemon pepper

1 Press Sauté button on Instant Pot® and add 2 tablespoons butter.

2 Place shrimp and salt in Instant Pot® and let cook 4 minutes until flesh is pink and opaque. Remove shrimp and set aside.

3 Pour in broth and deglaze bottom of pot.

4 Break spaghetti in half and place in pot. Top spaghetti with remaining 4 tablespoons butter.

5 Close lid and set pressure release to Sealing.

6 Press Manual or Pressure Cook button and adjust time to 5 minutes.

7 When the timer beeps, quick release pressure and then unlock lid and remove it.

8 Pour in cooked shrimp, cream, Parmesan, and lemon pepper. Mix until fully combined.

9 Serve hot.

PER SERVING

CALORIES: 966 | FAT: 48g | PROTEIN: 42g | SODIUM: 1,223mg
FIBER: 6g | CARBOHYDRATES: 91g | SUGAR: 4g

Lemon Pepper Tilapia "Bake"

Tender tilapia seasoned with lemon pepper and cooked alongside zucchini and yellow squash. The flavors in this fish bake meld together, making it a casserole unlike something you have tasted before!

- **Total Recipe Cost:** $3.62
- **Hands-On Time:** 10 minutes
- **Cook Time:** 11 minutes

Serves 4

1 cup water
½ pound tilapia fillets, cut into 2" chunks
1 medium yellow squash, sliced and halved
1 medium zucchini, sliced and halved
¼ cup grated Parmesan cheese
2 tablespoons olive oil
1 tablespoon lemon pepper
¾ teaspoon salt

1 Pour water into Instant Pot® and add trivet.

2 Combine tilapia, squash, zucchini, Parmesan, oil, lemon pepper, and salt in a 7" cake pan. Mix well. Cover pan tightly with foil.

3 Create a foil sling and carefully lower cake pan into Instant Pot®.

4 Close lid and set pressure release to Sealing.

5 Press Manual or Pressure Cook button and adjust time to 11 minutes.

6 When the timer beeps, quick release pressure and then unlock lid and remove it.

7 Remove cake pan using foil sling. Serve hot.

PER SERVING

CALORIES: 152 | FAT: 9g | PROTEIN: 14g | SODIUM: 558mg
FIBER: 1g | CARBOHYDRATES: 3g | SUGAR: 2g

Fish Tacos

Taco-seasoned cod served on corn tortillas and topped with a zesty sauce. We recommend serving it with chips and salsa on the side.

- **Total Recipe Cost: $7.92**
- **Hands-On Time: 15 minutes**
- **Cook Time: 5 minutes**

Serves 4

1 cup water
1 (1-ounce) packet taco seasoning
3 tablespoons olive oil
1 pound cod fillets
3 tablespoons mayonnaise
3 tablespoons full-fat sour cream
1 tablespoon lime juice
1 teaspoon sriracha
⅛ teaspoon garlic powder
⅛ teaspoon cumin
8 small corn tortillas
1 cup shredded red cabbage

1 Pour water into Instant Pot® and add trivet.

2 In a small bowl, mix together taco seasoning and oil. Brush taco seasoning on cod. Place seasoned cod on trivet.

3 Close lid and set pressure release to Sealing.

4 Press Manual or Pressure Cook button and adjust time to 5 minutes.

5 When the timer beeps, quick release pressure and then unlock lid and remove it. Remove cod.

6 In a small bowl, mix together mayonnaise, sour cream, lime juice, sriracha, garlic powder, and cumin.

7 Serve cod on tortillas topped with sauce and cabbage.

PER SERVING

CALORIES: 407 | **FAT:** 22g | **PROTEIN:** 24g | **SODIUM:** 745mg
FIBER: 5g | **CARBOHYDRATES:** 30g | **SUGAR:** 3g

Teriyaki Salmon

A flavor-packed salmon recipe that is ready in little time. The homemade teriyaki sauce really brings out the flavors of the salmon while the Instant Pot® keeps the fish perfectly tender. If in a pinch, bottled teriyaki sauce may be used in place of the homemade sauce.

- **Total Recipe Cost:** $5.51
- **Hands-On Time:** 5 minutes
- **Cook Time:** 0 minutes

Serves 4

1 pound salmon fillets

½ cup soy sauce

½ cup rice vinegar

½ cup packed light brown sugar

1 tablespoon cornstarch

1 teaspoon minced ginger

¼ teaspoon garlic powder

PRESSURE COOKING FOR 0 MINUTES

You may be wondering how you can cook a recipe for 0 minutes. It's simple, the Instant Pot® brings itself to pressure and immediately starts depressurizing again. The amount of time it takes to do this is the best way to cook salmon perfectly.

1 Place salmon in Instant Pot®.

2 In a small bowl, mix together soy sauce, rice vinegar, brown sugar, cornstarch, ginger, and garlic power. Pour over salmon, turning to coat.

3 Close lid and set pressure release to Sealing.

4 Press Manual or Pressure Cook button and adjust time to 0 minutes.

5 When the timer beeps, allow pressure to release naturally for 10 minutes and then quick release remaining pressure. Unlock lid and remove it.

6 Serve hot.

PER SERVING

CALORIES: 366 | **FAT:** 15g | **PROTEIN:** 26g | **SODIUM:** 1,833mg
FIBER: 0g | **CARBOHYDRATES:** 31g | **SUGAR:** 27g

Salmon Cakes

A tasty fish cake recipe with the flavors of green onion and soy sauce. These Salmon Cakes taste and look fancy. They can be served as a simple dinner or as an appetizer to wow your friends and family.

- **Total Recipe Cost:** $6.88
- **Hands-On Time:** 15 minutes
- **Cook Time:** 9 minutes

Serves 4

½ pound cooked salmon, shredded

2 large eggs

2 medium green onions, sliced

1 cup bread crumbs

½ cup flat leaf parsley, chopped

¼ cup soy sauce

1 tablespoon Worcestershire sauce

½ tablespoon garlic powder

1 teaspoon salt

½ teaspoon cayenne pepper

¼ teaspoon celery seed

4 tablespoons olive oil

1 In a large bowl, combine salmon, eggs, green onions, bread crumbs, parsley, soy sauce, Worcestershire, garlic powder, salt, cayenne, and celery seed. Mix together with clean hands until combined.

2 Press Sauté button on Instant Pot® and add oil.

3 Take golf ball–sized clumps of salmon mixture. Roll into balls and then flatten to form a cake. Place salmon cakes in an even layer in Instant Pot®.

4 Let cook 2 minutes until golden brown. Flip and cook an additional 2 minutes.

5 Repeat with remaining salmon mixture.

6 Store Salmon Cakes under foil until ready to serve.

PER SERVING

CALORIES: 402 | FAT: 25g | PROTEIN: 21g | SODIUM: 1,777mg
FIBER: 2g | CARBOHYDRATES: 24g | SUGAR: 3g

Lemon and Garlic Cod

A simple dish of cod, fresh lemon, and garlic. This recipe tastes great paired with Vegetable Tian (see recipe in Chapter 6).

- **Total Recipe Cost: $6.07**
- **Hands-On Time: 10 minutes**
- **Cook Time: 5 minutes**

Serves 4

1 pound cod fillets
1 medium lemon, cut into wedges
4 cloves garlic, smashed
½ teaspoon salt
¼ teaspoon black pepper
1 tablespoon olive oil
1 cup water

1 Place cod, lemon, and garlic in the center of a 1½' piece of foil. Season with salt and pepper. Drizzle with oil. Fold foil up on all sides to resemble a bowl and crimp edges tightly.

2 Place trivet and water in Instant Pot®. Carefully place foil packet on top of trivet.

3 Close lid and set pressure release to Sealing.

4 Press Manual or Pressure Cook button and adjust time to 5 minutes.

5 When the timer beeps, quick release pressure, and then unlock lid and remove it.

6 Remove foil packet from Instant Pot®. Carefully open foil packet; steam will release from inside.

7 Squeeze lemon over cod and serve.

PER SERVING

CALORIES: 130 | **FAT:** 4g | **PROTEIN:** 20g | **SODIUM:** 207mg
FIBER: 0g | **CARBOHYDRATES:** 2g | **SUGAR:** 0g

Tomato Basil Tilapia

The flavors of tomato and basil mingle perfectly with this mild whitefish.

- **Total Recipe Cost:** $4.63
- **Hands-On Time:** 10 minutes
- **Cook Time:** 2 minutes

Serves 4

1 pound tilapia fillets
½ teaspoon garlic powder
¼ teaspoon salt
⅛ teaspoon black pepper
½ (14.5-ounce) can diced
  tomatoes
1 tablespoon dried basil
1 tablespoon red wine
  vinegar
1 cup water

1 Place tilapia in the center of a 1½' piece of foil. Season with garlic powder, salt, and pepper.

2 In a small bowl, mix together tomatoes, basil, and vinegar.

3 Fold foil up on all sides of fish to resemble a bowl and pour in tomatoes. Crimp edges tightly around fish to create a foil packet.

4 Place trivet and water in Instant Pot®. Carefully place foil packet on top of trivet.

5 Close lid and set pressure release to Sealing.

6 Press Manual or Pressure Cook button and adjust time to 2 minutes.

7 When the timer beeps, quick release pressure and then unlock lid and remove it.

8 Remove foil packet from Instant Pot®. Carefully open foil packet; steam will release from inside.

9 Serve with tomatoes on top.

PER SERVING

CALORIES: 166 | **FAT:** 3g | **PROTEIN:** 31g | **SODIUM:** 306mg
FIBER: 1g | **CARBOHYDRATES:** 5g | **SUGAR:** 2g

Honey Garlic Salmon

Honey Garlic Salmon is a great way to serve salmon that tastes great and takes little time.

- **Total Recipe Cost:** $6.31
- **Hands-On Time:** 10 minutes
- **Cook Time:** 0 minutes

Serves 4

1 cup water
1 pound salmon fillets
½ teaspoon salt
¼ teaspoon black pepper
½ cup honey
4 tablespoons soy sauce
2 tablespoons rice vinegar
4 cloves garlic, minced
1 teaspoon sesame seeds

COOKING SALMON FROM FROZEN

It is easy to convert a fresh salmon recipe to a frozen salmon recipe. Simply add 2 minutes of cook time and natural pressure release as directed.

1 Pour water into Instant Pot® and add trivet.

2 Season salmon with salt and pepper and place on trivet.

3 Close lid and set pressure release to Sealing.

4 Press Manual or Pressure Cook button and adjust time to 0 minutes.

5 Once the timer beeps, allow pressure to release naturally for 10 minutes and then quick release remaining pressure. Unlock lid and remove it.

6 In a small bowl, whisk together honey, soy sauce, vinegar, garlic, and sesame seeds.

7 Pour sauce over salmon and serve.

PER SERVING

CALORIES: 356 | FAT: 13g | PROTEIN: 24g | SODIUM: 1,234mg
FIBER: 0g | CARBOHYDRATES: 37g | SUGAR: 35g

Spinach and Feta-Stuffed Tilapia

A fancier take on this mild whitefish. The spinach and feta cooks inside the tilapia, making it a cheesy and flavorful dish.

- **Total Recipe Cost:** $4.92
- **Hands-On Time:** 15 minutes
- **Cook Time:** 2 minutes

Serves 4

1 cup water
1 pound tilapia fillets
½ teaspoon salt
¼ teaspoon black pepper
1 cup baby spinach, chopped
2 ounces crumbled feta cheese
3 cloves garlic, minced

1 Pour water into Instant Pot® and add trivet.

2 Season tilapia with salt and pepper.

3 In a small bowl, combine spinach, feta, and garlic.

4 Fill the center of each tilapia fillet with the spinach mixture. Carefully roll up each fillet widthwise and secure with kitchen twine. Place rolled tilapia on trivet, seam-side up.

5 Close lid and set pressure release to Sealing.

6 Press Manual or Pressure Cook button and adjust time to 2 minutes.

7 When the timer beeps, quick release pressure and then unlock lid and remove it.

8 Cut twine on rolled tilapia and serve with seam-side down so the fish stays rolled.

PER SERVING

CALORIES: 188 | FAT: 6g | PROTEIN: 32g | SODIUM: 489mg
FIBER: 0g | CARBOHYDRATES: 2g | SUGAR: 1g

Chili Lime Tilapia

Chili powder and lime make a tasty combination. Rub it on tilapia and you have an easy and healthy meal ready for you.

- **Total Recipe Cost: $4.62**
- **Hands-On Time: 10 minutes**
- **Cook Time: 2 minutes**

Serves 4

1 cup water
4 tablespoons lime juice
3 tablespoons chili powder
½ teaspoon salt
1 pound tilapia fillets

1 Pour water into Instant Pot® and add trivet.

2 In a small bowl, whisk together lime juice, chili powder, and salt. Brush sauce onto both sides of tilapia fillets. Place tilapia on trivet.

3 Close lid and set pressure release to Sealing.

4 Press Manual or Pressure Cook button and adjust time to 2 minutes.

5 When the timer beeps, quick release pressure and then unlock lid and remove it.

6 Serve hot.

PER SERVING

CALORIES: 165 | FAT: 4g | PROTEIN: 31g | SODIUM: 529mg
FIBER: 2g | CARBOHYDRATES: 4g | SUGAR: 1g

Herb-Crusted Cod

All the flavor of fried fish made easily at home in your Instant Pot®. Make sure to use grated Parmesan for this recipe and not shredded as it affects the overall outcome of the crust.

- **Total Recipe Cost: $7.59**
- **Hands-On Time: 15 minutes**
- **Cook Time: 15 minutes**

Serves 4

1 pound cod fillets
1 teaspoon salt
½ teaspoon black pepper
1 cup whole milk
3 large eggs, lightly beaten
½ cup panko bread crumbs
¼ cup grated Parmesan
   cheese
1 tablespoon Italian
   seasoning
½ teaspoon garlic powder
6 tablespoons olive oil

FINDING THE BEST FISH PRICES

Purchasing frozen fish fillets is a great way to get the best value. We recommend purchasing 5-pound bags of individually frozen fillets. They can be found in the frozen seafood section of the grocery store. When ready to use, they can be easily defrosted in the refrigerator or by soaking in a container of tepid water.

1 Season cod with salt and pepper.

2 Set out three bowls; fill the first with milk, the second with eggs, and the third with panko.

3 To the panko, add Parmesan, Italian seasoning, and garlic powder and mix.

4 Press Sauté button on Instant Pot® and add oil.

5 Place cod fillet in bowl of milk. Take piece of cod from milk bowl and dip in egg. Shake off any excess egg and dip in panko.

6 Place panko-coated cod in hot oil.

7 Let cook until golden brown, about 3 minutes. Flip and cook an additional 3 minutes. Remove cod from Instant Pot® and place on a paper towel–lined plate.

8 Repeat with remaining fish.

9 Let cool slightly before serving.

PER SERVING

CALORIES: 423 | **FAT:** 28g | **PROTEIN:** 30g | **SODIUM:** 824mg **FIBER:** 1g | **CARBOHYDRATES:** 12g | **SUGAR:** 3g

Cajun Fish Cakes

A spin on the classic fish cake recipe, this recipe adds some heat and extra flavor.

- **Total Recipe Cost: $7.11**
- **Hands-On Time:** 15 minutes
- **Cook Time:** 15 minutes

Serves 4

1 pound cooked cod, shredded

1½ cups bread crumbs, divided

2 large eggs, lightly beaten

2 tablespoons full-fat sour cream

2 teaspoons lemon juice

1 tablespoon Cajun seasoning

4 tablespoons olive oil

1 In a large bowl, combine cod, bread crumbs, eggs, sour cream, lemon juice, and Cajun seasoning. Mix together with clean hands until combined.

2 Press Sauté button on Instant Pot® and add oil.

3 Take golf ball–sized clumps of cod mixture. Roll into balls and then flatten to form a cake. Place fish cakes in an even layer in Instant Pot®.

4 Let cook 2 minutes until golden brown. Flip and cook an additional 2 minutes.

5 Repeat with remaining cod mixture.

6 Store Cajun fish cakes under foil until ready to serve.

PER SERVING

CALORIES: 447 | FAT: 20g | PROTEIN: 35g | SODIUM: 423mg
FIBER: 2g | CARBOHYDRATES: 30g | SUGAR: 3g

Mini Tuna Casseroles

Have fun with your food. These Mini Tuna Casseroles are tasty and fun, thanks to the potato chips served on top!

- **Total Recipe Cost: $5.19**
- **Hands-On Time: 15 minutes**
- **Cook Time: 15 minutes**

Serves 6

1 cup water
1 (12-ounce) can tuna, drained and flaked
1 (10.5-ounce) can cream of mushroom soup
½ pound small shell pasta, cooked
1 cup shredded Cheddar cheese, divided
¾ cup frozen peas, thawed
¾ teaspoon salt
½ teaspoon garlic powder
½ teaspoon black pepper
24 potato chips

1 Pour water into Instant Pot® and add trivet.

2 In a large bowl, combine tuna, cream of mushroom soup, pasta, ½ cup Cheddar, peas, salt, garlic powder, and pepper. Mix.

3 Spray six ramekins with cooking spray.

4 Evenly divide tuna mixture into each ramekin and top with remaining cheese. Cover each ramekin tightly with foil and place on top of trivet, stacked two by two.

5 Close lid and set pressure release to Sealing.

6 Press Manual or Pressure Cook button and adjust time to 15 minutes.

7 When the timer beeps, quick release pressure and then unlock lid and remove it.

8 Carefully remove ramekins from Instant Pot® and remove foil.

9 Sprinkle four crushed-up potato chips over each casserole before serving.

PER SERVING

CALORIES: 381 | FAT: 15g | PROTEIN: 23g | SODIUM: 798mg
FIBER: 3g | CARBOHYDRATES: 39g | SUGAR: 3g

Vegetarian Main Dishes

You don't have to be a vegetarian to go meatless. Vegetarian main dishes are all about swapping out meat for hearty vegetables and potatoes. You are making healthy choices for your family while still enjoying a filling meal. We love cooking vegetarian dishes in the Instant Pot® because it cuts the cook-time down on dishes like Broccoli Cheddar "Baked" Potatoes while still delivering a flavorful meal.

Broccoli Potato Casserole

This simple dish of broccoli and mashed potatoes is a great way to use up leftover ingredients and repurpose them into a delicious and hearty casserole.

- **Total Recipe Cost: $4.04**
- **Hands-On Time:** 10 minutes
- **Cook Time:** 16 minutes

Serves 4

1 cup water
2 cups mashed potatoes
1 medium head broccoli, chopped
½ teaspoon salt
¼ teaspoon black pepper
¼ teaspoon garlic powder
1 cup shredded Cheddar cheese

ADDING A CRUNCHY TOPPING

If you want a crispy topping for the Broccoli Potato Casserole, try adding a cup of plain cornflakes on top. It adds a surprising crunch and texture to the dish.

1 Pour water into Instant Pot® and add trivet.

2 Spoon mashed potatoes into a 7" cake pan.

3 In a medium bowl, toss broccoli with salt, pepper, and garlic powder. Arrange seasoned broccoli on top of mashed potatoes.

4 Sprinkle cheese over broccoli. Cover cake pan tightly with foil.

5 Create a foil sling and carefully lower cake pan into Instant Pot®.

6 Close lid and set pressure release to Sealing.

7 Press Manual or Pressure Cook button and adjust time to 16 minutes.

8 When the timer beeps, quick release pressure and then unlock lid and remove it.

9 Remove cake pan using foil sling and then remove foil from top of pan and serve.

PER SERVING

CALORIES: 275 | FAT: 13g | PROTEIN: 13g | SODIUM: 896mg
FIBER: 6g | CARBOHYDRATES: 29g | SUGAR: 3g

Black Bean and Corn-Stuffed Peppers

This vegetarian take on stuffed peppers is still hearty and filling thanks to the protein-packed black beans.

- **Total Recipe Cost: $6.33**
- **Hands-On Time:** 10 minutes
- **Cook Time:** 8 minutes

Serves 4

1 cup water
½ (15.25-ounce) can black beans, rinsed and drained
1 (4-ounce) can mild diced green chilies
1 cup cooked rice
1 cup frozen corn kernels, thawed
4 large green bell peppers
½ cup shredded Cheddar cheese

1 Pour water into Instant Pot® and place trivet inside.

2 In a medium bowl, mix together beans, green chilies, rice, and corn. Set aside.

3 Slice tops of bell peppers off and remove seeds from inside peppers.

4 Scoop black bean mixture into each pepper and fill just to the top.

5 Carefully place stuffed peppers inside Instant Pot® so they are standing upright on trivet.

6 Close lid and set pressure release to Sealing.

7 Press Manual or Pressure Cook button and adjust time to 8 minutes.

8 When the timer beeps, quick release pressure and then unlock lid and remove it.

9 Remove peppers and sprinkle with cheese. Serve hot.

PER SERVING

CALORIES: 237 | FAT: 6g | PROTEIN: 11g | SODIUM: 400mg
FIBER: 7g | CARBOHYDRATES: 37g | SUGAR: 9g

Skinny Alfredo Pasta with Carrots and Broccoli

A lightened-up version of the classic Alfredo pasta recipe. This dish is still creamy and delicious with less fat and calories. We swapped out meat for vegetables, making it a filling vegetarian meal.

- **Total Recipe Cost: $7.03**
- **Hands-On Time: 10 minutes**
- **Cook Time: 12 minutes**

Serves 4

2 tablespoons olive oil
1 medium head broccoli, chopped
3 medium carrots, sliced
2 cloves garlic, minced
½ teaspoon salt
½ teaspoon black pepper
¼ teaspoon onion powder
4 cups vegetable broth
1 pound fettuccine
2 tablespoons butter, cubed
1 cup whole milk
¾ cup grated Parmesan cheese
½ cup cold water
1 tablespoon cornstarch

1 Press Sauté button on Instant Pot® and add oil. Place broccoli and carrots in Instant Pot®. Let cook, stirring occasionally, 5 minutes.

2 Add garlic, salt, pepper, and onion powder. Cook an additional 30 seconds.

3 Pour in broth and deglaze bottom of pot. Break fettuccine in half and place in pot. Top fettuccine with cubed butter.

4 Close lid and set pressure release to Sealing.

5 Press Manual or Pressure Cook button and adjust time to 6 minutes.

6 When the timer beeps, quick release pressure and then unlock lid and remove it.

7 Pour in milk and Parmesan and mix until fully combined.

8 In a small bowl, whisk together water and cornstarch. Mix into Alfredo pasta and stir for 1 minute.

9 Serve hot.

PER SERVING

CALORIES: 733 | FAT: 22g | PROTEIN: 29g | SODIUM: 721mg
FIBER: 11g | CARBOHYDRATES: 107g | SUGAR: 12g

Black Bean and Rice Casserole

Eating beans and rice for dinner can save you money, but it doesn't have to be boring. This flavorful casserole will make your budget and your belly happy.

- **Total Recipe Cost: $2.31**
- **Hands-On Time:** 10 minutes
- **Cook Time:** 8 minutes

Serves 4

1 cup water
2 cups cooked brown rice
1 (15.25-ounce) can black beans
1 (15-ounce) can sweet corn kernels
1 (4-ounce) can mild diced green chilies
½ teaspoon salt
½ teaspoon dried oregano
½ teaspoon cumin
½ teaspoon red pepper flakes

1 Pour water into Instant Pot® and add trivet.

2 In a 6-cup metal bowl, combine rice, black beans, corn, chilies, salt, oregano, cumin, and red pepper flakes and mix. Cover bowl tightly with foil.

3 Create a foil sling and carefully lower bowl into Instant Pot®.

4 Close lid and set pressure release to Sealing.

5 Press Manual or Pressure Cook button and adjust time to 8 minutes.

6 When the timer beeps, quick release pressure and then unlock lid and remove it.

7 Remove bowl using foil sling and then remove foil from bowl and serve.

PER SERVING

CALORIES: 294 | FAT: 2g | PROTEIN: 12g | SODIUM: 1,064mg
FIBER: 11g | CARBOHYDRATES: 62g | SUGAR: 8g

Honey and Garlic "Baked" Cauliflower

This dish is reminiscent of Chinese takeout with cauliflower as the main protein instead of chicken or pork.

- **Total Recipe Cost:** $5.91
- **Hands-On Time:** 15 minutes
- **Cook Time:** 6 minutes

Serves 4

1 cup water

1 medium head cauliflower, chopped

1 cup all-purpose flour

4 large eggs, lightly beaten

1 cup panko bread crumbs

9 tablespoons honey

6 cloves garlic, minced

4 tablespoons soy sauce

1½ tablespoons hot chili sauce

1 Pour water into Instant Pot® and add trivet.

2 Place cauliflower and flour in a gallon-sized zip-topped bag. Shake until cauliflower is evenly coated with flour.

3 Dip each piece of cauliflower into eggs and then into bread crumbs. Place coated cauliflower in a 6-cup metal bowl.

4 Inside the Instant Pot®, combine honey, garlic, soy sauce, and hot chili sauce. Press Sauté and let simmer 1 minute, stirring constantly.

5 Pour sauce over cauliflower in the metal bowl. Cover bowl of cauliflower tightly with foil.

6 Clean inner pot and place back inside Instant Pot®. Create a foil sling and carefully lower bowl into Instant Pot®.

7 Close lid and set pressure release to Sealing.

8 Press Manual or Pressure Cook button and adjust time to 5 minutes.

9 When the timer beeps, quick release pressure and then unlock lid and remove it.

10 Remove bowl using foil sling. Take foil off of top of bowl and serve.

PER SERVING

CALORIES: 453 | FAT: 6g | PROTEIN: 16g | SODIUM: 1,031mg
FIBER: 5g | CARBOHYDRATES: 88g | SUGAR: 43g

Sweet Potato Enchilada Casserole

This casserole is an unrolled version of enchiladas filled with sweet potatoes, black beans, and bell pepper.

- **Total Recipe Cost:** $5.41
- **Hands-On Time:** 10 minutes
- **Cook Time:** 14 minutes

Serves 4

2 tablespoons olive oil

½ medium sweet potato, peeled and diced

½ medium yellow onion, peeled and diced

½ medium red bell pepper, seeded and diced

½ teaspoon salt

¼ teaspoon red pepper flakes

¼ teaspoon dried oregano

¼ teaspoon black pepper

2 cloves garlic, minced

1 (15.25-ounce) can black beans, drained and rinsed

1 (10-ounce) can red enchilada sauce

4 small corn tortillas

1 cup shredded Cheddar cheese

1 cup water

1 Press Sauté button and add oil. Add sweet potato, onion, bell pepper, salt, red pepper flakes, oregano, and black pepper. Cook until sweet potatoes are tender, about 5 minutes.

2 Add garlic and black beans. Cook an additional 30 seconds. Turn Instant Pot® off.

3 Pour half can of enchilada sauce on bottom of 7" cake pan. Place one tortilla over sauce.

4 Scoop one third sweet potato mixture over tortilla and top with another tortilla. Continue for remaining filling and tortillas. Top enchiladas with remaining ½ can sauce and cheese. Cover cake pan tightly with foil.

5 Clean inner pot and place back inside Instant Pot®. Pour water into Instant Pot® and add trivet.

6 Create foil sling and carefully lower cake pan into Instant Pot®.

7 Close lid and set pressure release to Sealing.

8 Press Manual or Pressure Cook button and adjust time to 8 minutes.

9 When the timer beeps, quick release pressure and then unlock lid and remove it.

10 Remove pan using foil sling and then remove foil from pan and serve.

PER SERVING

CALORIES: 372 | FAT: 17g | PROTEIN: 16g | SODIUM: 1,242mg
FIBER: 9g | CARBOHYDRATES: 40g | SUGAR: 7g

Cheesy Ravioli Casserole

This simple and delicious casserole features layers of ravioli, cheese, and pasta sauce. Any variety of ravioli can be used in this recipe. A great alternate would be spinach ravioli.

- **Total Recipe Cost:** $3.71
- **Hands-On Time:** 10 minutes
- **Cook Time:** 10 minutes

Serves 2

1 cup water
1 cup pasta sauce, divided
1 (9-ounce) package cheese ravioli, cooked
½ cup ricotta cheese
¼ cup Parmesan cheese
1 tablespoon finely chopped Italian parsley

1 Pour water into Instant Pot® and add trivet.

2 Spread ¼ cup pasta sauce on bottom of 7" cake pan.

3 Arrange cooked ravioli in cake pan. Drop spoonfuls of ricotta cheese over ravioli, some ravioli may still peak through.

4 Pour remaining ¾ cup pasta sauce over ravioli and ricotta. Sprinkle Parmesan and parsley over casserole. Cover cake pan tightly with foil.

5 Create a foil sling and carefully lower cake pan into Instant Pot®.

6 Close lid and set pressure release to Sealing.

7 Press Manual or Pressure Cook button and adjust time to 10 minutes.

8 When the timer beeps, quick release pressure and then unlock lid and remove it.

9 Remove cake pan using foil sling and then remove foil from cake pan and serve.

PER SERVING

CALORIES: 405 | **FAT:** 20g | **PROTEIN:** 23g | **SODIUM:** 1,622mg
FIBER: 3g | **CARBOHYDRATES:** 35g | **SUGAR:** 5g

Spinach Lasagna Rolls

These delicious lasagna rolls are filled with creamy ricotta and chopped spinach. They come out perfectly moist every time, thanks to the Instant Pot®.

- **Total Recipe Cost:** $6.27
- **Hands-On Time:** 15 minutes
- **Cook Time:** 12 minutes

Serves 4

1 cup water
1 (15-ounce) container ricotta cheese
1 cup chopped spinach
½ cup grated Parmesan cheese, divided
4 cloves garlic, minced
1 large egg, lightly beaten
½ teaspoon salt
¼ teaspoon black pepper
1¼ cups pasta sauce, divided
8 lasagna noodles, cooked

CAN OVEN-READY LASAGNA NOODLES BE USED?

Oven-ready lasagna noodles are wonderful for saving time while making lasagna. Unfortunately, they cannot be used for this recipe. The noodles must be precooked in order to roll them.

1 Pour water into Instant Pot® and add trivet.

2 In a large bowl, combine ricotta, spinach, ¼ cup Parmesan, garlic, egg, salt, and pepper. Mix well.

3 Spread ¼ cup pasta sauce on bottom of 7" cake pan.

4 Lay cooked lasagna noodles out flat and spread ricotta filling on top of each noodle, keeping filling inside edges of noodles. Roll each lasagna noodle up lengthwise and arrange inside cake pan.

5 Spread remaining sauce over lasagna rolls and top with remaining Parmesan cheese. Tightly cover cake pan with foil.

6 Create a foil sling and carefully lower cake pan into Instant Pot®.

7 Close lid and set pressure release to Sealing.

8 Press Manual or Pressure Cook button and adjust time to 12 minutes.

9 When the timer beeps, quick release pressure and then unlock lid and remove it.

10 Remove pan using foil sling and then remove foil from pan and serve.

PER SERVING

CALORIES: 485 | FAT: 19g | PROTEIN: 27g | SODIUM: 936mg
FIBER: 4g | CARBOHYDRATES: 51g | SUGAR: 4g

Tomato Basil Tortellini

A one-pot pasta dish that's packed full of tomato basil flavor. If in a pinch, 2 tablespoons dried basil may be used in place of fresh basil.

- **Total Recipe Cost: $7.20**
- **Hands-On Time: 5 minutes**
- **Cook Time:** 10 minutes

Serves 4

4 quarts water
¾ teaspoon salt, divided
1 (19-ounce) package frozen cheese tortellini
2 tablespoons olive oil
1 pint grape tomatoes
4 tablespoons finely chopped basil
2 cloves garlic, minced
½ teaspoon red pepper flakes
¼ teaspoon black pepper
½ cup grated Parmesan cheese

1 Press Sauté button on Instant Pot®. Pour in water and ½ teaspoon salt. Bring to a boil.

2 Pour in tortellini and boil 3 minutes until tortellini floats to top of water. Drain water, reserving 1 cup water. Remove tortellini and set aside.

3 Add oil to Instant Pot® and add tomatoes. Cook, stirring occasionally, until tomatoes begin to burst about 5 minutes.

4 Add basil, garlic, red pepper, black pepper, and remaining ¼ teaspoon salt. Stir and cook 30 seconds.

5 Pour in reserved water, tortellini, and Parmesan cheese. Stir 30 seconds.

6 Serve hot.

PER SERVING

CALORIES: 538 | FAT: 20g | PROTEIN: 24g | SODIUM: 940mg
FIBER: 4g | CARBOHYDRATES: 68g | SUGAR: 3g

Broccoli Cheddar "Baked" Potatoes

This recipe calls for cooking the potatoes and then adding the broccoli at the end with a pressure cook time of 0 minutes. If your lid does not want to go back onto the Instant Pot® when adding the broccoli, wait 1 minute and try again.

- **Total Recipe Cost:** $4.22
- **Hands-On Time:** 10 minutes
- **Cook Time:** 13 minutes

Serves 4

1 cup water
4 medium russet potatoes
1 medium head broccoli, chopped
½ teaspoon salt
¼ teaspoon black pepper
1 cup shredded Cheddar cheese

WANT CRISPIER SKIN?

If you want your potatoes to have the crispy baked potato skin, place the cooked potatoes on a baking pan. Spray with cooking spray and sprinkle with ½ teaspoon salt. Place potatoes under broiler for 3 minutes until the skins begin to crisp up.

1 Pour water into Instant Pot® and add trivet.

2 Pierce each potato four times with tines of a fork. Place potatoes on top of trivet.

3 Close lid and set pressure release to Sealing.

4 Press Manual or Pressure Cook button and adjust time to 12 minutes.

5 When the timer beeps, quick release pressure and then unlock lid and remove it.

6 Place steamer basket in Instant Pot®, on top of potatoes. Arrange broccoli inside steamer basket.

7 Close lid and set pressure release to Sealing.

8 Press Manual or Pressure Cook button and adjust time to 0 minutes.

9 When the timer beeps, quick release pressure and then unlock lid and remove it.

10 Remove broccoli and potatoes.

11 Slice each potato open and season with salt and pepper. Top each potato with broccoli and cheese. Serve.

PER SERVING

CALORIES: 334 | FAT: 10g | PROTEIN: 15g | SODIUM: 391mg
FIBER: 7g | CARBOHYDRATES: 50g | SUGAR: 4g

Mushroom Risotto

This Instant Pot® risotto with mushroom and Parmesan is a quick and easy way to make risotto without all of the hands-on time in front of the stove.

- **Total Recipe Cost: $9.94**
- **Hands-On Time: 10 minutes**
- **Cook Time: 11 minutes**

Serves 4

4 tablespoons olive oil
4 tablespoons butter, divided
1 medium yellow onion, peeled and diced
4 cloves garlic, minced
2 cups sliced mushrooms
1½ cups arborio rice
4 cups vegetable broth
1 cup grated Parmesan cheese
1 teaspoon dried parsley
½ teaspoon salt
¼ teaspoon black pepper

1 Press Sauté button on Instant Pot®. Add oil and 2 tablespoons butter to Instant Pot®. Add onion and cook 3 minutes.

2 Add garlic and cook an additional 30 seconds.

3 Mix in mushrooms and rice. Pour in broth and deglaze bottom of pot. Turn Instant Pot® off.

4 Close lid and set pressure release to Sealing.

5 Press Manual or Pressure Cook button and adjust time to 7 minutes.

6 When the timer beeps, quick release pressure and then unlock lid and remove it.

7 Mix in remaining 2 tablespoons butter, Parmesan cheese, dried parsley, salt, and pepper.

8 Serve hot.

PER SERVING

CALORIES: 579 | FAT: 31g | PROTEIN: 14g | SODIUM: 700mg
FIBER: 3g | CARBOHYDRATES: 67g | SUGAR: 5g

Broccoli Cheese Risotto

A fun twist on risotto made with tender broccoli and flavorful cheese.

- **Total Recipe Cost:** $7.11
- **Hands-On Time:** 10 minutes
- **Cook Time:** 12 minutes

Serves 4

4 tablespoons olive oil

4 tablespoons butter, divided

1 medium head broccoli, chopped

4 cloves garlic, minced

1½ cups arborio rice

4 cups vegetable broth

1 cup shredded Cheddar cheese

½ teaspoon salt

¼ teaspoon black pepper

1 Press Sauté button on Instant Pot®. Add oil and 2 tablespoons butter to Instant Pot®. Add broccoli and cook 4 minutes.

2 Add garlic and cook an additional 30 seconds. Remove broccoli and garlic. Set aside.

3 Add rice to Instant Pot® and stir.

4 Pour in broth and deglaze bottom of pot. Turn Instant Pot® off.

5 Close lid and set pressure release to Sealing.

6 Press Manual or Pressure Cook button and adjust time to 7 minutes.

7 When the timer beeps, quick release pressure and then unlock lid and remove it.

8 Mix in broccoli and garlic, remaining 2 tablespoons butter, Cheddar cheese, salt, and pepper.

9 Serve hot.

PER SERVING

CALORIES: 643 | FAT: 36g | PROTEIN: 16g | SODIUM: 592mg
FIBER: 6g | CARBOHYDRATES: 73g | SUGAR: 6g

Sun-Dried Tomato Pesto Pasta

Whip up this fresh and flavorful meal for an easy weeknight dinner.

- **Total Recipe Cost: $7.49**
- **Hands-On Time: 15 minutes**
- **Cook Time: 4 minutes**

Serves 4

6 cups water

1 pound penne pasta

1 teaspoon salt, divided

1 (8-ounce) jar sun-dried tomatoes packed in olive oil

1 small bunch fresh basil

¾ cup grated Parmesan cheese, divided

3 cloves garlic

½ teaspoon black pepper

1 In Instant Pot®, combine water, pasta, and ¼ teaspoon salt.

2 Close lid and set pressure release to Sealing.

3 Press Manual or Pressure Cook button and adjust time to 4 minutes.

4 When the timer beeps, quick release pressure and then unlock lid and remove it. Drain water.

5 In the bowl of a food processor, combine sun-dried tomatoes, basil, ½ cup Parmesan, garlic, pepper, and remaining ¾ teaspoon salt. Process until smooth, about 30 seconds.

6 Pour pesto and remaining ¼ cup Parmesan into pot of pasta.

7 Mix and serve.

PER SERVING

CALORIES: 651 | FAT: 8g | PROTEIN: 30g | SODIUM: 900mg
FIBER: 12g | CARBOHYDRATES: 119g | SUGAR: 23g

Sweet Potato Risotto

Creamy risotto paired with hearty sweet potato makes a tasty meal with little hands-on time.

- **Total Recipe Cost: $8.24**
- **Hands-On Time:** 10 minutes
- **Cook Time:** 13 minutes

Serves 4

4 tablespoons olive oil

4 tablespoons butter, divided

1 medium shallot, peeled and diced

1 medium sweet potato, cut into small chunks

4 cloves garlic, minced

1½ cups arborio rice

4 cups vegetable broth

½ teaspoon salt

¼ teaspoon black pepper

WHERE IS THE WINE?
Many risotto recipes call for cooking the rice in one part dry white wine. If you prefer the flavor of wine in your risotto, simply swap out 1 cup broth for 1 cup dry white wine and follow all steps as written in the recipe.

1 Press Sauté button on Instant Pot®. Add oil and 2 tablespoons butter. Add shallot and sweet potatoes. Cook, stirring occasionally, 5 minutes.

2 Add garlic and rice and cook an additional 30 seconds.

3 Pour in broth and deglaze bottom of pot. Turn Instant Pot® off.

4 Close lid and set pressure release to Sealing.

5 Press Manual or Pressure Cook button and adjust time to 7 minutes.

6 When the timer beeps, quick release pressure and then unlock lid and remove it.

7 Mix in remaining 2 tablespoons butter, salt, and pepper.

8 Serve hot.

PER SERVING

CALORIES: 512 | FAT: 26g | PROTEIN: 6g | SODIUM: 377mg
FIBER: 3g | CARBOHYDRATES: 71g | SUGAR: 5g

Creamy Vegetable Medley

A combination of carrots, broccoli, and cauliflower, tossed in a creamy sauce. You won't miss the meat in this recipe because the hearty vegetables are filling enough on their own.

- **Total Recipe Cost: $7.64**
- **Hands-On Time: 10 minutes**
- **Cook Time: 1 minute**

Serves 4

1 pound carrots, sliced
1 medium head cauliflower, chopped
1 medium head broccoli, chopped
2 cups water
1 cup heavy whipping cream
½ cup grated Parmesan cheese
1 teaspoon salt
¾ teaspoon black pepper

1 Place carrots in Instant Pot®. Top with cauliflower and then broccoli. Pour water over vegetables.

2 Close lid and set pressure release to Sealing.

3 Press Manual or Pressure Cook button and adjust time to 1 minutes.

4 When the timer beeps, quick release pressure and then unlock lid and remove it.

5 Drain water.

6 Pour in cream, Parmesan, salt, and pepper. Mix 1 minute until vegetables are evenly coated with sauce and cheese is melted.

7 Serve hot.

PER SERVING

CALORIES: 380 | FAT: 26g | PROTEIN: 14g | SODIUM: 1,376mg
FIBER: 10g | CARBOHYDRATES: 30g | SUGAR: 13g

Corn and Black Bean Quesadillas

Crispy flour tortillas filled with the perfect combination of black beans, corn, and cheese.

- **Total Recipe Cost: $7.06**
- **Hands-On Time: 10 minutes**
- **Cook Time: 24 minutes**

Serves 4

½ (15.25-ounce) can black beans
½ (15-ounce) can corn
½ (4-ounce) can mild diced green chilies
4 tablespoons unsalted butter, divided
8 (10") flour tortillas
4 cups grated Mexican-blend cheese

1 In a medium bowl, mix together black beans, corn, and green chilies.

2 Press Sauté button on Instant Pot® and add 1 tablespoon butter. Once butter is melted, place one tortilla in Instant Pot®.

3 Spread one quarter of black bean mixture on top of tortilla. Add 1 cup shredded cheese and top with another tortilla. Cook until bottom tortilla starts to brown, about 3 minutes.

4 Carefully flip quesadilla over and continue to cook until the other tortilla has started to brown and the cheese has melted, another 3 minutes.

5 Repeat with three remaining quesadillas, starting with 1 tablespoon butter for each quesadilla.

6 Cut each quesadilla into triangles and serve.

PER SERVING

CALORIES: 1,121 | FAT: 63g | PROTEIN: 45g | SODIUM: 2,915mg
FIBER: 10g | CARBOHYDRATES: 95g | SUGAR: 12g

Macaroni and Cheese

This is the Macaroni and Cheese recipe of your dreams! It's perfectly creamy and loaded with two different kinds of cheese.

- **Total Recipe Cost:** $7.20
- **Hands-On Time:** 10 minutes
- **Cook Time:** 4 minutes

Serves 4

1 pound elbow macaroni

4 cups water

2 tablespoons hot sauce

2 cups heavy cream

2 cups shredded Cheddar cheese

2 cups shredded Monterey jack cheese

1 Combine macaroni, water, and hot sauce in Instant Pot®.

2 Close lid and set pressure release to Sealing.

3 Press Manual or Pressure Cook button and adjust time to 4 minutes.

4 When the timer beeps, quick release pressure and then unlock lid and remove it.

5 Mix in cream and cheeses. Stir 1 minute until cheese is melted. Serve.

PER SERVING

CALORIES: 949 | FAT: 80g | PROTEIN: 34g | SODIUM: 786mg
FIBER: 1g | CARBOHYDRATES: 25g | SUGAR: 4g

WHY HOT SAUCE?

If you are not a fan of spicy foods, don't let the addition of hot sauce turn you off. The hot sauce does not add heat to this dish, but it does add flavor. It is an important ingredient and should not be skipped.

11

Desserts

One of the best things you can do in your Instant Pot® is make dessert. Not only does the Instant Pot® make the best cheesecakes, but it makes amazing crisps, cobblers, and cakes too! Nothing gets dried out when cooking in the Instant Pot®.

Cherry Cobbler

You need this Cherry Cobbler in your life! The canned cherry pie filling saves time and makes it easy to serve at any time of year. A mixture of granulated and brown sugar may be substituted in the cobbler for a deeper flavor. For best results, make this cobbler recipe ahead of time and let it cool completely before serving.

- **Total Recipe Cost:** $4.06
- **Hands-On Time:** 10 minutes
- **Cook Time:** 30 minutes

Serves 6

1½ cups water
1 (20-ounce) can cherry pie filling
¾ cup granulated sugar
¾ cup all-purpose flour
⅛ teaspoon salt
6 tablespoons unsalted butter, melted
1 teaspoon vanilla extract

WHY IS MY COBBLER DOUGH SO SOFT?

When you remove your cobbler from the Instant Pot®, you may notice it's still soft on top. This is completely normal. The cobbler will firm up as it cools to room temperature. This is why it is so important to let the dessert cool to room temperature before serving.

1 Pour water into Instant Pot® and add trivet. Grease a 7" cake pan with cooking spray.

2 Pour cherry pie filling into cake pan.

3 In a medium bowl, mix together sugar, flour, and salt.

4 Slowly drizzle melted butter and vanilla into bowl. Mix together with a fork until mixture is wet.

5 With clean hands, grab clumps of the cobbler dough and squeeze into a ball. Then flatten into a round.

6 Place dough rounds on top of cherry pie filling. Continue making rounds with the cobbler dough and arrange slightly overlapped on top of cherry pie filling. Tightly cover cake pan with foil.

7 Create a foil sling and slowly lower cherry cobbler into Instant Pot®.

8 Close lid and set pressure release to Sealing.

9 Press Manual or Pressure Cook button and adjust time to 30 minutes.

10 When the timer beeps, quick release pressure and then unlock lid and remove it.

11 Remove cake pan using foil sling and then remove foil from top of cake pan. Let cool to room temperature before serving.

PER SERVING

CALORIES: 372 | FAT: 12g | PROTEIN: 2g | SODIUM: 100mg
FIBER: 1g | CARBOHYDRATES: 64g | SUGAR: 49g

Peach Cobbler

We love this recipe because it uses canned peaches—making it possible to enjoy year-round. If you have fresh peaches on hand, they may be used in place of canned; just peel and slice the peaches until you have 3 cups' worth and toss with 1 tablespoon lemon juice.

- **Total Recipe Cost: $4.01**
- **Hands-On Time: 15 minutes**
- **Cook Time: 35 minutes**

Serves 6

1 cup water
2 (14.5-ounce) cans cling peaches, drained
¾ cup plus 3 tablespoons granulated sugar, divided
3 tablespoons packed light brown sugar
½ tablespoon cornstarch
½ teaspoon ground cinnamon
1½ teaspoons vanilla extract, divided
¾ cup all-purpose flour
⅛ teaspoon salt
6 tablespoons unsalted butter, melted

1 Pour water into Instant Pot® and add trivet.

2 Inside a 7″ cake pan, combine peaches, 3 tablespoons granulated sugar, brown sugar, cornstarch, cinnamon, and ½ teaspoon vanilla. Mix until combined.

3 In a medium bowl, mix together remaining ¾ cup sugar, flour, and salt.

4 Slowly drizzle melted butter and remaining 1 teaspoon vanilla into medium bowl. Mix together with a fork until mixture is wet.

5 With clean hands, grab clumps of the cobbler dough and squeeze into a ball. Then flatten into a round.

6 Place rounds on top of peaches. Continue making rounds with the cobbler dough and arrange slightly overlapped on top of peaches. Tightly cover cake pan with foil.

7 Create a foil sling and slowly lower pan into Instant Pot®.

8 Close lid and set pressure release to Sealing.

9 Press Manual or Pressure Cook button and adjust time to 35 minutes.

10 When the timer beeps, quick release pressure and then unlock lid and remove it.

11 Remove cake pan using foil sling. Remove foil from top of cake pan. Let cool completely to room temperature before serving.

PER SERVING

CALORIES: 378 | FAT: 12g | PROTEIN: 2g | SODIUM: 58mg
FIBER: 2g | CARBOHYDRATES: 68g | SUGAR: 51g

Berry Crisp

A triple-berry dessert topped with a sweet crisp. Try pairing this with vanilla bean ice cream!

- **Total Recipe Cost:** $1.87
- **Hands-On Time:** 15 minutes
- **Cook Time:** 8 minutes

Serves 6

1 cup water
2 cups frozen mixed berries, thawed
½ cup granulated sugar
½ tablespoon cornstarch
½ cup all-purpose flour
½ cup old-fashioned rolled oats
⅓ cup packed light brown sugar
⅛ teaspoon salt
4 tablespoons unsalted butter, melted

1 Pour water into Instant Pot® and add trivet. Grease a 7" cake pan.

2 Fill cake pan with berries, granulated sugar, and cornstarch. Mix.

3 In a medium bowl, mix together flour, oats, brown sugar, and salt.

4 Slowly mix in melted butter using a fork. Mix until butter is well combined with dry ingredients.

5 Sprinkle crisp topping over berries. Cover cake pan tightly with foil.

6 Create a foil sling and carefully lower cake pan into Instant Pot®.

7 Close lid and set pressure release to Sealing.

8 Press Manual or Pressure Cook button and adjust time to 8 minutes.

9 When the timer beeps, quick release pressure and then unlock lid and remove it.

10 Carefully remove pan using foil sling and remove foil from pan.

11 Let cool on a cooling rack. Serve at room temperature.

PER SERVING

CALORIES: 267 | FAT: 8g | PROTEIN: 2g | SODIUM: 54mg
FIBER: 2g | CARBOHYDRATES: 47g | SUGAR: 32g

Cookies and Cream Cheesecake

This cheesecake is the best of both worlds—a creamy cheesecake filled with crunchy chocolate cookies.

- **Total Recipe Cost: $5.62**
- **Hands-On Time: 15 minutes**
- **Cook Time: 40 minutes**

Serves 6

1 cup water
26 cream-filled chocolate sandwich cookies, divided
2 tablespoons unsalted butter, melted
16 ounces cream cheese, softened
½ cup granulated sugar
1 teaspoon vanilla extract
½ cup full-fat sour cream
2 large eggs, room temperature

USE CARE WHEN ADDING THE EGGS

It is important to not overmix the eggs in your cheesecake. When you overmix the eggs, you introduce air into the batter, which result in cracks in the top of your cheesecake. If using an electric mixer, they should be mixed for only 10 seconds per egg.

1 Pour water into Instant Pot® and add trivet. Grease a 7″ PushPan and set aside.

2 Place 16 chocolate cookies in a gallon-sized zip-top bag and seal. Roll with a rolling pin until small crumbs are formed.

3 In a small bowl, mix crushed cookies and melted butter together.

4 Press cookie crust into bottom and halfway up sides of greased PushPan. Place pan in freezer while preparing cheesecake batter.

5 With an electric mixer, cream together cream cheese, sugar, and vanilla. Beat until light and fluffy, about 2 minutes.

6 Slowly add in sour cream and mix.

7 Add in eggs, one at a time, beating after each addition. Only mix until combined. Do not overmix.

8 Chop remaining cookies and fold half of them into cheesecake batter. Reserve remaining chopped cookies for topping.

9 Pour batter into PushPan. Create a foil sling and carefully lower pan into Instant Pot®.

10 Close lid and set pressure release to Sealing.

11 Press Manual or Pressure Cook button and adjust time to 40 minutes.

12 When the timer beeps, allow pressure to release naturally and then unlock lid and remove it.

13 Carefully remove pan from Instant Pot® using foil sling. Place on a cooling rack and let cool to room temperature.

continued on next page

Cookies and Cream Cheesecake (continued)

14 Cover with plastic wrap and refrigerate for a minimum of 8 hours.

15 Top cheesecake with remaining chopped cookies and serve.

PER SERVING

CALORIES: 642 | **FAT:** 44g | **PROTEIN:** 10g | **SODIUM:** 452mg
FIBER: 1g | **CARBOHYDRATES:** 56g | **SUGAR:** 40g

Peanut Butter Cup Cheesecake

The perfect combination of peanut butter and chocolate wrapped into a cheesecake featuring a chocolate ganache and a peanut butter cup topping.

- **Total Recipe Cost: $9.68**
- **Hands-On Time: 15 minutes**
- **Cook Time: 40 minutes**

Serves 6

1 cup water

16 cream-filled chocolate sandwich cookies

2 tablespoons unsalted butter, melted

16 ounces cream cheese, softened

¾ cup packed light brown sugar

½ cup heavy whipping cream, divided

½ cup creamy peanut butter

1¼ teaspoons vanilla extract, divided

2 large eggs, room temperature

24 mini peanut butter cups, divided and chopped

½ cup semisweet chocolate chips

1 Pour water into Instant Pot® and add trivet. Grease a 7" PushPan and set aside.

2 Place chocolate cookies in a gallon-sized zip-top bag and seal. Roll with a rolling pin until small crumbs are formed.

3 In a small bowl, mix crushed cookies and melted butter together. Press cookie crust into bottom and halfway up sides of greased PushPan. Place pan in freezer while preparing cheesecake batter.

4 With an electric mixer, cream together cream cheese and brown sugar. Beat until light and fluffy, about 2 minutes.

5 Mix in $1/4$ cup cream, peanut butter, and 1 teaspoon vanilla. Mix an additional 2 minutes.

6 Add in eggs, one at a time, beating until just combined. Do not overmix.

7 Fold in half of the chopped peanut butter cups. Pour batter into PushPan.

8 Create a foil sling and carefully lower pan into Instant Pot®.

9 Close lid and set pressure release to Sealing.

10 Press Manual or Pressure Cook button and adjust time to 40 minutes.

11 When the timer beeps, allow pressure to release naturally and then unlock lid and remove it.

12 Carefully remove pan from Instant Pot® using foil sling. Place on a cooling rack and let cool to room temperature.

continued on next page

Peanut Butter Cup Cheesecake
(continued)

13   Remove water from Instant Pot® and press Sauté button.

14   Pour remaining $1/4$ cup cream into Instant Pot® and heat until steaming.

15   Place chocolate chips and remaining $1/4$ teaspoon vanilla in a small bowl and then pour warm cream over them and stir. Let sit 5 minutes until chocolate is melted. Stir until combined. Pour this ganache over cheesecake.

16   Refrigerate for a minimum of 8 hours.

17   Top cheesecake with remaining chopped peanut butter cups and serve.

PER SERVING

CALORIES: 806 | **FAT:** 51g | **PROTEIN:** 15g | **SODIUM:** 345mg
FIBER: 4g | **CARBOHYDRATES:** 79g | **SUGAR:** 63g

Chocolate Hazelnut Lava Cakes

Cakey on the outside and gooey on the inside. These mini lava cakes are the perfect chocolate dessert. It is important to time this dessert so it may be served quickly after cooking so the center stays moist and chocolaty.

- **Total Recipe Cost:** $4.40
- **Hands-On Time:** 15 minutes
- **Cook Time:** 11 minutes

Serves 4

1 cup water
½ cup unsalted butter, melted
½ cup granulated sugar
3 large eggs
1 teaspoon vanilla extract
1 cup chocolate hazelnut spread
¼ cup all-purpose flour
¼ cup semisweet chocolate chips

1 Pour water into Instant Pot® and add trivet. Grease four ramekins and set aside.

2 With an electric mixer, cream together butter and sugar. Mix 2 minutes until light and fluffy.

3 Mix in eggs and vanilla, one at a time, beating after each addition.

4 Add hazelnut spread and beat until fully combined.

5 Mix in flour and continue mixing until all dry spots are gone. Fold in chocolate chips.

6 Divide cake batter evenly among ramekins. Cover each ramekin tightly with foil.

7 Place each ramekin in Instant Pot®, three on bottom and the fourth on top, stacked in the center of the three.

8 Close lid and set pressure release to Sealing.

9 Press Manual or Pressure Cook button and adjust time to 11 minutes.

10 When the timer beeps, quick release pressure and then unlock lid and remove it.

11 Carefully remove ramekins from Instant Pot®, using an oven mitt. Let sit 5 minutes before serving.

12 If serving lava cakes outside of ramekins is desired, run a butter knife around the edges of the cake and carefully turn over on a plate.

PER SERVING

CALORIES: 826 | FAT: 51g | PROTEIN: 10g | SODIUM: 88mg
FIBER: 5g | CARBOHYDRATES: 83g | SUGAR: 70g

Red Velvet Cake

A simple chocolate cake made with cream cheese frosting. The Bundt pan makes it beautiful.

- **Total Recipe Cost: $5.95**
- **Hands-On Time: 20 minutes**
- **Cook Time: 32 minutes**

Serves 6

1 cup water
¾ cup vegetable oil
¾ cup granulated sugar
2 large eggs
2 teaspoons vanilla extract, divided
1¼ cups cake flour
3 tablespoons unsweetened cocoa powder
½ teaspoon salt
½ cup buttermilk
1 teaspoon red gel food coloring
1 teaspoon baking soda
1 teaspoon white vinegar
4 ounces cream cheese, softened
¼ cup unsalted butter, softened
2 cups powdered sugar, sifted

1. Pour water into Instant Pot® and add trivet. Grease a 6-cup Bundt pan and set aside.
2. With an electric mixer, cream together oil and sugar, 2 minutes.
3. Add eggs and 1 teaspoon vanilla, one at a time, beating after each addition.
4. In a medium bowl, whisk together flour, cocoa powder, and salt.
5. Slowly add flour mixture and buttermilk to the mixer, alternating between the two until fully combined.
6. Pour in food coloring and mix until batter turns red.
7. In a small bowl, combine baking soda and vinegar. Give it a quick stir (it will start to bubble) and pour into cake batter. Mix an additional 10 seconds.
8. Pour cake batter into greased Bundt pan. Create a foil sling and carefully lower Bundt pan into Instant Pot®.
9. Close lid and set pressure release to Sealing.
10. Press Manual or Pressure Cook button and adjust time to 32 minutes.
11. When the timer beeps, quick release pressure and then unlock lid and remove it.
12. Carefully remove Bundt pan using foil sling and let cool on a cooling rack.
13. With an electric mixer, cream together cream cheese and butter. Mix until light and fluffy, about 4 minutes.

Red Velvet Cake (continued)

14 Slowly mix in powdered sugar and remaining vanilla. Continue mixing until a fluffy frosting is formed, about 2 minutes.

15 Once cake is cooled, run a butter knife around inner and outer edges of cake. Turn cake over onto a plate and wiggle to remove Bundt pan.

16 Spread cream cheese frosting over cake and serve.

PER SERVING

CALORIES: 620 | **FAT:** 44g | **PROTEIN:** 7g | **SODIUM:** 510mg
FIBER: 1g | **CARBOHYDRATES:** 51g | **SUGAR:** 27g

Mini Pumpkin Cheesecakes

All the creamy and tasty flavor of pumpkin cheesecake in a mini form. These cheesecakes are cooked in ramekins—the perfect serving dish—making cleanup easy.

- **Total Recipe Cost: $3.87**
- **Hands-On Time: 15 minutes**
- **Cook Time: 13 minutes**

Serves 4

1 cup water
12 gingersnap cookies
½ cup plus 1 tablespoon granulated sugar, divided
¼ teaspoon salt, divided
2 tablespoons unsalted butter, melted
12 ounces cream cheese, softened
½ cup pure canned pumpkin
1 teaspoon vanilla extract
¼ teaspoon ground cinnamon
⅛ teaspoon ground nutmeg
⅛ teaspoon allspice
1 large egg plus 1 large egg yolk, room temperature

1 Pour water into Instant Pot® and add trivet. Grease four ramekins and set aside.

2 Place gingersnap cookies, 1 tablespoon sugar, and ⅛ teaspoon salt in a gallon-sized zip-top bag and seal. Roll with a rolling pin until small crumbs are formed.

3 In a small bowl, mix crushed cookies and melted butter together.

4 Press cookie crust into bottom of ramekins. Place ramekins in freezer while preparing cheesecake batter.

5 With an electric mixer, cream together cream cheese and remaining ½ cup sugar. Beat until light and fluffy, about 2 minutes.

6 Mix in pumpkin, vanilla, cinnamon, nutmeg, allspice, and remaining ⅛ teaspoon salt. Mix an additional 2 minutes.

7 Add in egg and egg yolk, one at a time, and beat until just combined. Do not overmix.

8 Divide batter evenly among four ramekins. Cover each ramekin tightly with foil.

9 Place each ramekin in Instant Pot®, three on bottom and the fourth on top, stacked in the center of the three.

10 Close lid and set pressure release to Sealing.

11 Press Manual or Pressure Cook button and adjust time to 13 minutes.

12 When the timer beeps, allow pressure to release naturally and then unlock lid and remove it.

Mini Pumpkin Cheesecakes
(continued)

13 Carefully remove ramekins from Instant Pot®, using an oven mitt. Place on a cooling rack and let cool to room temperature.

14 Refrigerate at least 8 hours before serving.

PER SERVING

CALORIES: 589 | FAT: 40g | PROTEIN: 9g | SODIUM: 540mg
FIBER: 1g | CARBOHYDRATES: 52g | SUGAR: 37g

Pineapple Upside-Down Cake

Sweet, caramelized pineapples prepared with a sweet yellow cake. This cake comes out beautifully and tastes great.

- **Total Recipe Cost:** $5.78
- **Hands-On Time:** 15 minutes
- **Cook Time:** 32 minutes

Serves 6

1 cup water
1 (8-ounce) can pineapple slices
12 maraschino cherries, stems removed
⅓ cup packed light brown sugar
½ cup plus 2 tablespoons unsalted butter, softened
1 cup granulated sugar
2 large eggs plus 1 large egg yolk
2 teaspoons vanilla extract
1½ cups cake flour
2 teaspoons baking powder
¼ teaspoon salt
¾ cup buttermilk

1 Pour water into Instant Pot® and add trivet. Grease a 7" cake pan.

2 Arrange pineapple slices in a single layer on bottom of cake pan, breaking slices in half to fit, as needed. Reserve pineapple juice. Place cherries in openings of pineapple slices.

3 Sprinkle brown sugar over pineapples and cherries.

4 Cut 2 tablespoons butter into small chunks and arrange over brown sugar.

5 With an electric mixer, cream together remaining ½ cup butter and granulated sugar. Mix until fluffy, about 2 minutes.

6 Add eggs and egg yolk, one at a time, beating after each addition. Mix in vanilla.

7 In a separate medium bowl, combine flour, baking powder, and salt. Mix.

8 Slowly mix flour mixture and buttermilk into wet mixture, alternating between flour and buttermilk until ingredients are fully combined.

9 Pour cake batter into cake pan. Cover cake pan tightly with foil. Create a foil sling and carefully lower pan into Instant Pot®.

10 Close lid and set pressure release to Sealing.

11 Press Manual or Pressure Cook button and adjust time to 32 minutes.

12 When the timer beeps, quick release pressure and then unlock lid and remove it.

continued on next page

Pineapple Upside-Down Cake
(continued)

13 Carefully remove cake pan from Instant Pot® using foil sling. Remove foil from top of pan.

14 Use a straw to poke twenty holes in cake. Pour reserved pineapple juice on top of cake. Let sit on a cooling rack about 30 minutes.

15 Run a knife around edges of cake. Turn cake over onto a plate to remove from pan.

16 Let cool to room temperature and serve.

PER SERVING

CALORIES: 566 | **FAT:** 23g | **PROTEIN:** 7g | **SODIUM:** 283mg
FIBER: 1g | **CARBOHYDRATES:** 85g | **SUGAR:** 57g

Apple Crisp

Want to make a delicious apple dessert with all of the fresh apples you have on hand? The recipe calls for Gala apples, but any favorite apple varieties may be used. Keep in mind that tart apples will make a more tart crisp.

- **Total Recipe Cost:** $3.11
- **Hands-On Time:** 15 minutes
- **Cook Time:** 8 minutes

Serves 6

1 cup water
3 medium Gala apples, peeled, cored, and sliced
¼ cup granulated sugar
1 tablespoon lemon juice
½ teaspoon ground cinnamon
⅓ cup packed brown sugar
½ cup all-purpose flour
½ cup old-fashioned rolled oats
⅛ teaspoon salt
2 tablespoons unsalted butter, melted

FREEZING CRISPS AND COBBLERS

Crisps and cobblers are very freezer friendly. You will want to cook them as directed and let them cool completely to room temperature. Then you can choose to leave them in their cake pan or transfer to another, freezer-friendly container. Wrap them tightly in two layers of foil and freeze up to three months. Defrost in the refrigerator before serving.

1 Pour water into Instant Pot® and add trivet. Grease a 7″ cake pan.

2 Toss apples, granulated sugar, lemon juice, and cinnamon in cake pan. Mix until combined.

3 In a medium bowl, mix together brown sugar, flour, oats, and salt.

4 Slowly mix in melted butter using a fork. Mix until butter is well combined with dry ingredients. Sprinkle crisp topping over apples.

5 Cover cake pan tightly with foil. Create a foil sling and carefully lower cake pan into Instant Pot®.

6 Close lid and set pressure release to Sealing.

7 Press Manual or Pressure Cook button and adjust time to 8 minutes.

8 When the timer beeps, quick release pressure and then unlock lid and remove it.

9 Carefully remove pan using foil sling and remove foil from pan. Let cool on a cooling rack.

10 Serve at room temperature.

PER SERVING

CALORIES: 216 | FAT: 5g | PROTEIN: 2g | SODIUM: 53mg
FIBER: 2g | CARBOHYDRATES: 44g | SUGAR: 29g

Brownies

Make a batch of these fudgy Brownies in your Instant Pot®. Simply slice them up like a cake when ready to serve.

- **Total Recipe Cost:** $3.20
- **Hands-On Time:** 15 minutes
- **Cook Time:** 50 minutes

Serves 6

1½ cups water
½ cup unsalted butter, softened
1 cup granulated sugar
2 large eggs
1 teaspoon vanilla extract
½ cup all-purpose flour
⅓ cup unsweetened cocoa powder
¼ teaspoon baking powder
¼ teaspoon salt
½ cup semisweet chocolate chips

WANT FROSTED BROWNIES?

If you have your heart set on frosted brownies, simply whisk together 1 cup powdered sugar (sifted), ¼ cup softened butter, ⅛ cup whole milk, 3 tablespoons unsweetened cocoa powder, and 1 teaspoon vanilla extract. Mix until the frosting is light and fluffy. Spread over hot brownies and let cool as directed.

1. Pour water into Instant Pot® and add trivet. Grease a 7″ cake pan and set aside.

2. With an electric mixer, cream together butter and sugar. Mix until light and fluffy, about 2 minutes.

3. Mix in eggs and vanilla, one at a time, beating after each addition.

4. In a medium bowl, mix together flour, cocoa powder, baking powder, and salt.

5. Slowly mix dry ingredients into wet ingredients. Fold in chocolate chips.

6. Pour brownie batter into greased cake pan. Cover pan tightly with foil. Create a foil sling and carefully lower cake pan into Instant Pot®.

7. Close lid and set pressure release to Sealing.

8. Press Manual or Pressure Cook button and adjust time to 50 minutes.

9. When the timer beeps, allow pressure to release naturally and then unlock lid and remove it.

10. Carefully remove cake pan using foil sling. Remove foil from pan.

11. Let Brownies cool on a cooling rack to room temperature before serving.

PER SERVING

CALORIES: 408 | FAT: 22g | PROTEIN: 5g | SODIUM: 141mg
FIBER: 3g | CARBOHYDRATES: 54g | SUGAR: 41g

Coconut Caramel Cake

This sweet cake made with a yellow cake base and topped with chocolate ganache, caramel, and coconut is a total winner. It tastes and looks great!

- **Total Recipe Cost: $7.55**
- **Hands-On Time: 20 minutes**
- **Cook Time: 32 minutes**

Serves 6

1½ cups water
½ cup unsalted butter, softened
1 cup granulated sugar
2 large eggs plus 1 large egg yolk
3 teaspoons vanilla extract, divided
1½ cups cake flour
2 teaspoons baking powder
¼ teaspoon salt
¾ cup buttermilk
1 (12.25-ounce) container caramel topping, divided
¼ cup heavy whipping cream
½ cup chocolate chips
1 cup sweetened coconut flakes, toasted

HOW TO TOAST COCONUT?

Toasting coconut is relatively easy and can be done in the Instant Pot® or on the stovetop. Simple heat a skillet to medium-high heat or press the Sauté button and let the Instant Pot® heat up for 3 minutes. Pour coconut into pot and stir occasionally, 5 minutes, until coconut is golden brown.

1 Pour water into Instant Pot® and add trivet. Grease a 7" cake pan.

2 With an electric mixer, cream together butter and granulated sugar. Mix until fluffy, about 2 minutes.

3 Add eggs and egg yolk, one at a time, beating after each addition. Mix in 2 teaspoons vanilla.

4 In a separate medium bowl, combine flour, baking powder, and salt.

5 Slowly mix flour mixture and buttermilk into wet mixture, alternating between flour and buttermilk until ingredients are fully combined.

6 Fold in half of caramel topping.

7 Pour cake batter into cake pan. Cover cake pan tightly with foil. Create a foil sling and carefully lower pan into Instant Pot®.

8 Close lid and set pressure release to Sealing.

9 Press Manual or Pressure Cook button and adjust time to 32 minutes.

10 When the timer beeps, quick release pressure and then unlock lid and remove it.

11 Carefully remove cake pan from Instant Pot® using foil sling. Remove foil from top of pan. Let cake cool 30 minutes on cooling rack.

12 Run a knife around edges of cake. Turn cake over onto a plate to remove from pan.

13 Remove water from Instant Pot® and press Sauté button. Pour in cream and heat until steaming.

continued on next page

Coconut Caramel Cake (continued)

14 Place chocolate chips and remaining 1 teaspoon vanilla in a small bowl. Pour heated cream over chocolate chips. Mix once and let sit 5 minutes. Stir until smooth.

15 Pour two thirds of chocolate ganache over top of cake. Top with remaining caramel topping and then sprinkle with toasted coconut. Top cake with remaining one third of chocolate ganache.

16 Let cake continue to cool an additional 10 minutes before serving.

PER SERVING

CALORIES: 739 | **FAT:** 31g | **PROTEIN:** 9g | **SODIUM:** 520mg
FIBER: 3g | **CARBOHYDRATES:** 112g | **SUGAR:** 82g

Chocolate-Dipped Strawberries

These delicious treats are quick and easy with the Instant Pot® used as a double boiler. You can roll them in festive sprinkles for a holiday-inspired treat.

- **Total Recipe Cost: $5.74**
- **Hands-On Time: 5 minutes**
- **Cook Time: 5 minutes**

Serves 8

2 cups water
½ cup chocolate sprinkles
1 cup semisweet chocolate chips
2 tablespoons coconut oil
1 pound strawberries with stems

1 Pour water in Instant Pot® and press Sauté button. Let water come to a boil. Lay out a piece of parchment paper next to Instant Pot®. Place sprinkles into a small shallow bowl.

2 Once water is boiling, add trivet with a 6-cup metal bowl on top.

3 Add chocolate chips and coconut oil to bowl. Let sit 5 minutes until melted.

4 Give chocolate a stir to make sure it is fully combined with oil. Turn Instant Pot® off and then press Keep Warm button.

5 Holding strawberry stem, dip it into melted chocolate and then sprinkles.

6 Lay dipped strawberry on parchment paper and continue with remaining strawberries.

7 Let strawberries cool, 10 minutes, before serving.

PER SERVING

CALORIES: 204 | FAT: 13g | PROTEIN: 1g | SODIUM: 3mg
FIBER: 3g | CARBOHYDRATES: 25g | SUGAR: 21g

Cherry Chocolate Poke Cake

A delicious chocolate cake with the cherry flavoring added right into the cake and on top of the chocolate frosting.

- **Total Recipe Cost: $6.13**
- **Hands-On Time: 20 minutes**
- **Cook Time: 32 minutes**

Serves 6

1 cup water
¾ cup vegetable oil
¾ cup granulated sugar
2 large eggs
2 teaspoons vanilla extract, divided
1¼ cups cake flour
6 tablespoons unsweetened cocoa powder, divided
½ teaspoon salt
½ cup buttermilk
1 teaspoon baking soda
1 teaspoon white vinegar
1 (10-ounce) jar maraschino cherries, chopped and divided with juice reserved
1 cup powdered sugar, sifted
¼ cup unsalted butter, softened
⅛ cup whole milk

1 Pour water into Instant Pot® and add trivet. Grease a 6-cup Bundt pan and set aside.

2 With an electric mixer, cream together oil and sugar. Mix 2 minutes.

3 Add eggs and 1 teaspoon vanilla, one at a time, beating after each addition.

4 In a medium bowl, whisk together flour, 3 tablespoons cocoa powder, and salt.

5 Slowly add flour mixture and buttermilk to the egg mixture, alternating between the two until fully combined.

6 In a small bowl, combine baking soda and vinegar. Give it a quick stir (it will start to bubble) and pour into cake batter. Mix an additional 10 seconds.

7 Fold in half of the chopped maraschino cherries. Pour cake batter into greased Bundt pan. Create a foil sling and carefully lower Bundt pan into Instant Pot®.

8 Close lid and set pressure release to Sealing.

9 Press Manual or Pressure Cook button and adjust time to 32 minutes.

10 When the timer beeps, quick release pressure and then unlock lid and remove it. Carefully remove Bundt pan using foil sling.

11 Use a straw to poke twenty holes in cake. Pour cherry juice into holes. Place cake on cooling rack and let cool, about 30 minutes.

continued on next page

Cherry Chocolate Poke Cake
(continued)

12 With an electric mixer, mix together pow-
    dered sugar, butter, remaining 3 table-
    spoons cocoa powder, milk, and remaining
    1 teaspoon vanilla. Mix until light and fluffy,
    about 2 minutes.

13 Once cake is cooled, run a butter knife
    around inner and outer edges of cake.
    Turn cake over onto a plate and wiggle to
    remove Bundt pan.

14 Spread chocolate frosting on top of cake
    and top with remaining cherries.

PER SERVING

CALORIES: 716 | **FAT:** 38g | **PROTEIN:** 6g | **SODIUM:** 305mg
FIBER: 4g | **CARBOHYDRATES:** 92g | **SUGAR:** 64g

Lemon Cheesecake

This creamy cheesecake is made with a traditional graham cracker crust and a hint of lemon flavoring. Its kept perfectly moist thanks to the water in the Instant Pot®.

- **Total Recipe Cost: $3.45**
- **Hands-On Time: 15 minutes**
- **Cook Time: 40 minutes**

Serves 6

1 cup water

6 graham crackers

⅓ cup plus 2 tablespoons granulated sugar, divided

⅛ teaspoon salt

3 tablespoons unsalted butter, melted

16 ounces cream cheese, softened

1 teaspoon vanilla extract

3 tablespoons lemon juice

1 tablespoon lemon zest

1 large egg plus 1 large egg yolk

1 Pour water into Instant Pot® and add trivet. Grease a 7" PushPan and set aside.

2 Place graham crackers, 2 tablespoons sugar, and salt in a gallon-sized zip-top bag and seal. Roll with a rolling pin until small crumbs are formed.

3 In a small bowl, mix crushed graham crackers and melted butter together. Press graham cracker crust into bottom and halfway up sides of greased PushPan. Place pan in freezer.

4 With an electric mixer, cream together cream cheese and remaining ⅓ cup sugar. Beat until light and fluffy, about 2 minutes.

5 Mix in vanilla, lemon juice, and lemon zest. Beat an additional 1 minute.

6 Add in egg and egg yolk, one at a time, beating until just combined. Do not overmix.

7 Pour batter into PushPan. Create a foil sling and carefully lower pan into Instant Pot®.

8 Close lid and set pressure release to Sealing.

9 Press Manual or Pressure Cook button and adjust time to 40 minutes.

10 When the timer beeps, allow pressure to release naturally and then unlock lid and remove it.

11 Carefully remove pan from Instant Pot® using foil sling. Place on a cooling rack and let cool to room temperature.

12 Refrigerate for a minimum of 8 hours. Serve chilled.

PER SERVING

CALORIES: 357 | FAT: 34g | PROTEIN: 6g | SODIUM: 318mg
FIBER: 0g | CARBOHYDRATES: 8g | SUGAR: 4g

Cinnamon Apples

This simple apple dish tastes like apple pie without the crust. It's an uncomplicated dessert that could easily be whipped together on a weeknight.

- **Total Recipe Cost: $5.90**
- **Hands-On Time: 10 minutes**
- **Cook Time: 5 minutes**

Serves 4

1 cup water

3 medium Granny Smith apples, peeled and sliced

3 medium Gala apples, peeled and sliced

½ cup packed light brown sugar

2 tablespoons lemon juice

2 teaspoons ground cinnamon

½ teaspoon ground nutmeg

1 Pour water into Instant Pot® and add trivet.

2 In a 6-cup metal bowl, toss together apples, brown sugar, lemon juice, cinnamon, and nutmeg.

3 Cover bowl tightly with foil. Create a foil sling and carefully lower bowl into Instant Pot®.

4 Close lid and set pressure release to Sealing.

5 Press Manual or Pressure Cook button and adjust time to 5 minutes.

6 When the timer beeps, quick release pressure and then unlock lid and remove it.

7 Remove bowl using foil sling. Remove foil lid and stir apples. Serve warm.

PER SERVING

CALORIES: 227 | FAT: 0g | PROTEIN: 1g | SODIUM: 8mg
FIBER: 4g | CARBOHYDRATES: 60g | SUGAR: 51g

Easy White Cake

Save time by using a boxed cake mix. Your favorite flavor of cake mix can be swapped out and used in this recipe.

- **Total Recipe Cost: $3.20**
- **Hands-On Time: 10 minutes**
- **Cook Time: 35 minutes**

Serves 6

2 cups water, divided
1 (15.25-ounce) box white cake mix
3 large eggs
⅓ cup vegetable oil
1 (16-ounce) container frosting

1 Pour 1 cup water into Instant Pot® and add trivet. Grease a 6-cup Bundt pan and set aside.

2 In a large bowl, mix together cake mix, eggs, oil, and remaining 1 cup water. Pour cake batter into Bundt pan.

3 Make a foil sling and carefully lower Bundt pan into Instant Pot®.

4 Close lid and set pressure release to Sealing.

5 Press Manual or Pressure Cook button and adjust time to 35 minutes.

6 When the timer beeps, quick release pressure and then unlock lid and remove it.

7 Remove Bundt pan using foil sling and let cool on a cooling rack 1 hour.

8 Once cake is cooled, run a butter knife around inner and outer edges of cake. Turn cake over onto a plate and wiggle to remove Bundt pan.

9 Spread frosting on top of cake and serve.

PER SERVING

CALORIES: 814 | **FAT:** 40g | **PROTEIN:** 7g | **SODIUM:** 649mg
FIBER: 0g | **CARBOHYDRATES:** 107g | **SUGAR:** 79g

Double Chocolate Zucchini Bread

It's important not to drain the zucchini for this recipe; the liquid adds moisture.

- **Total Recipe Cost: $4.68**
- **Hands-On Time: 15 minutes**
- **Cook Time: 65 minutes**

Serves 6

1 cup water
1½ cups all-purpose flour
1 cup granulated sugar
½ cup cocoa powder
½ teaspoon ground cinnamon
½ teaspoon baking soda
½ teaspoon baking powder
½ teaspoon salt
2 large eggs
½ cup vegetable oil
1 teaspoon vanilla extract
1 cup shredded zucchini
½ cup semisweet chocolate chips

1 Grease and flour a 7" PushPan. Pour water into Instant Pot® and add trivet.

2 In a large bowl, whisk together flour, sugar, cocoa powder, cinnamon, baking soda, baking powder, and salt.

3 In a medium bowl, whisk together eggs, vegetable oil, and vanilla.

4 Make a well in center of dry ingredients and pour in wet ingredients. Mix until combined. Fold in zucchini and chocolate chips.

5 Pour batter into prepared PushPan. Place a paper towel on top of pan and tightly cover with foil.

6 Create a foil sling and gently lower pan into Instant Pot®. Close lid and set pressure release to Sealing.

7 Press Manual or Pressure Cook button and adjust time to 65 minutes.

8 When the timer beeps, quick release pressure, unlock lid and remove it, and carefully remove bread using foil sling.

9 Remove foil and paper towel. Use a clean paper towel to gently blot up any additional moisture that may have accumulated.

10 Let cool on a cooling rack 10 minutes. Remove using push feature in pan.

11 Store any leftovers in an air-tight container up to three days.

PER SERVING

CALORIES: 517 | **FAT:** 25g | **PROTEIN:** 8g | **SODIUM:** 358mg
FIBER: 5g | **CARBOHYDRATES:** 72g | **SUGAR:** 42g

US/Metric Conversion Chart

VOLUME CONVERSIONS

US Volume Measure	Metric Equivalent
⅛ teaspoon	0.5 milliliter
¼ teaspoon	1 milliliter
½ teaspoon	2 milliliters
1 teaspoon	5 milliliters
½ tablespoon	7 milliliters
1 tablespoon (3 teaspoons)	15 milliliters
2 tablespoons (1 fluid ounce)	30 milliliters
¼ cup (4 tablespoons)	60 milliliters
⅓ cup	90 milliliters
½ cup (4 fluid ounces)	125 milliliters
⅔ cup	160 milliliters
¾ cup (6 fluid ounces)	180 milliliters
1 cup (16 tablespoons)	250 milliliters
1 pint (2 cups)	500 milliliters
1 quart (4 cups)	1 liter (about)

WEIGHT CONVERSIONS

US Weight Measure	Metric Equivalent
½ ounce	15 grams
1 ounce	30 grams
2 ounces	60 grams
3 ounces	85 grams
¼ pound (4 ounces)	115 grams
½ pound (8 ounces)	225 grams
¾ pound (12 ounces)	340 grams
1 pound (16 ounces)	454 grams

OVEN TEMPERATURE CONVERSIONS

Degrees Fahrenheit	Degrees Celsius
200 degrees F	95 degrees C
250 degrees F	120 degrees C
275 degrees F	135 degrees C
300 degrees F	150 degrees C
325 degrees F	160 degrees C
350 degrees F	180 degrees C
375 degrees F	190 degrees C
400 degrees F	205 degrees C
425 degrees F	220 degrees C
450 degrees F	230 degrees C

BAKING PAN SIZES

American	Metric
8 x 1½ inch round baking pan	20 x 4 cm cake tin
9 x 1½ inch round baking pan	23 x 3.5 cm cake tin
11 x 7 x 1½ inch baking pan	28 x 18 x 4 cm baking tin
13 x 9 x 2 inch baking pan	30 x 20 x 5 cm baking tin
2 quart rectangular baking dish	30 x 20 x 3 cm baking tin
15 x 10 x 2 inch baking pan	30 x 25 x 2 cm baking tin (Swiss roll tin)
9 inch pie plate	22 x 4 or 23 x 4 cm pie plate
7 or 8 inch springform pan	18 or 20 cm springform or loose bottom cake tin
9 x 5 x 3 inch loaf pan	23 x 13 x 7 cm or 2 lb narrow loaf or pâté tin
1½ quart casserole	1.5 liter casserole
2 quart casserole	2 liter casserole

Index

Note: Page numbers in **bold** indicate recipe category lists.

The cookbook that makes using your *Instant Pot*® easier than ever!

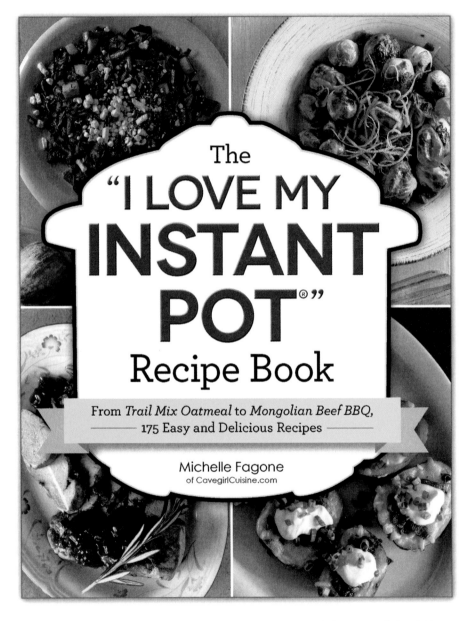

The "I LOVE MY INSTANT POT®" Recipe Book

From *Trail Mix Oatmeal* to *Mongolian Beef BBQ*, 175 Easy and Delicious Recipes

Michelle Fagone
of CavegirlCuisine.com

PICK UP OR DOWNLOAD YOUR COPY TODAY!

adamsmedia
An Imprint of Simon & Schuster
A CBS COMPANY